"The writing program has given me s⦿
discuss my fears without judgment; a gⁱ   g;
and a great community of support
so very helpful in healing the spirit!"
—Rick C.

"This group has saved my life. When I first came to the group, I was raw from
hearing a dire diagnosis, chemo scarred and exhausted. The writing group
gave me somewhere to go. A reason to get up in the morning. A reason to
get dressed. A reason to leave the house. A place of connection. A place of
wisdom. A place of welcome. A place of peace. I won't get the gift of a cure in
my lifetime, but I receive the healing gifts of story and of being heard every
week. It's a good dose. It's the best dose. And I attribute a degree of my
vitality these days to the healing power of the stories we weave."
—Amy P.

"We give and receive hope, wisdom, strength, understanding,
and even love. It has made me feel more supported and less alone
during the scariest year of my life."
—Hillary H.

"Writing group is far more than a support group. It's the highlight
of my week. My fellow young adult writing group members are now my dear
friends and I can't think of a more enjoyable way to spend an evening."
—Juliana P.

"The opportunity to write about my cancer journey and my life has been
inspiring, instructional, and spiritual. I find myself looking for writing
prompts everywhere, which translates into finding grace and gratitude in
the midst of sorrow and suffering and uncertainty. The connection with
other women writers is both supportive and inspirational. Especially during
the pandemic, that connection is a sacred lifeline."
—Bonnie F.

We Become a New Story

*Writing from
Women, Men & Young Adults
Healing from Cancer*

Patient & Family Services • KNIGHT CANCER *Institute*

Editors: Dawn Thompson & Ash Good

Copy Editor: Rick M. Cook

Cover Artist: Marti Price Morten

Interior Illustrations: Deborah Brod

ISBN 979-8-218-12183-9

WWW.OHSU.EDU/KNIGHT-CANCER-INSTITUTE

Contents

a sympathy note to my body

into the dark forest

hang on in this moment for the ride

come with us and fly

Origins of the OHSU Writing Groups

In the early 2000s, I was an Assistant Professor in the Department of Surgery conducting breast cancer research. After decades of pursuing laboratory research, I wanted a better understanding of the clinical aspects of this disease. This moved me into the operating room and the Multidisciplinary Breast Clinic for the next year. In the clinic, I observed the clinical team interacting with patients, where results of physical examinations, as well as radiology and pathology, were conveyed. I witnessed the delivery of compassionate and excellent medical care. However, the diagnosis was at times very complex, unanticipated, and sometimes carried an emotionally devastating message.

What I remember most vividly and what had the greatest impact on the creation of the cancer writing group was my experience of watching patients leaving the clinic following their appointment with their results in hand and a follow-up appointment set. While the next medical action might have been concrete for them, the emotional path that they would have to navigate was far from defined. It was clear to me that while we were offering excellent medical care, it appeared crucial to explore new avenues for additional emotional support to assist patients with the challenging journey they were now embarking upon. Storytelling came to mind.

While exploring different ideas, I learned of the Amherst Writers & Artists group. This association was formed to encourage and assist writers to develop their authentic voice through storytelling. Their method proved useful in various forums where the voices and words of authors had been suppressed or underrepresented. To me, it seemed that in the setting where it is often difficult to openly discuss cancer, a writing group designed in the AWA format would provide a safe space for exploring one's cancer journey. I made several trips to Amherst to learn how to facilitate AWA writing groups and how I might apply them to a medical care facility, specifically in the context of working with patients with cancer.

I adapted the AWA style of writing, which utilizes a presented prompt to inspire the process of storytelling, and designed a repeating ten-week course that would address many of the experiences that are common to people newly diagnosed with cancer. Every person's cancer experience is unique, but there are common medical milestones that patients journey through. As such, the ten-week course was designed to meet weekly and present a prompt that focused on that milestone.

The initial groups were developed for women exclusively. Groups designed for men or adolescents and youth came along in the later years. I approached the Center for Women's Health who graciously provided the physical space for our groups to meet for several years. The Stimson-Miller Foundation generously provided funding for the groups and the financial support that allowed me to expand the group's leadership to include facilitators beyond myself. Nearly two decades later, it is a joy to me that the OHSU Knight Cancer Institute writing group is still ongoing and providing a healing space for people experiencing cancer.

—SuEllen J. Pommier, Ph.D, M.Div.

Associate Professor Emeritus, Oregon Health & Science University
Ordained minister and chaplain, Episcopal Diocese of Oregon

The Healing Art of Writing

As James Pennebaker wrote in *Opening Up: The Healing Power of Expressing Emotions,* there is benefit to putting emotionally upsetting experiences into words. He notes that writing can clear the mind, help in acquiring and remembering new information, foster problem solving, and—some would suggest—bolster the immune system. Not unlike psychotherapy, writing can yield improvements in psychological and physical health. The value of writing or talking about our thoughts and feelings lies in reducing inhibition and organizing our complicated mental and emotional lives.

When I was invited to return to Oregon Health & Sciences University in 2011 to develop a program of services for the Knight Cancer Institute, I thought about the distress that a cancer diagnosis brings to most patients and their loved ones. Having been an oncology social worker for more than three decades, I was well aware that "one size" does not fit all when it comes to the provision of support for our patients. Additionally, it is known that approximately 50% of Americans add some sort of "complementary" care to their traditional medical care. "Complementary care" can include approaches such as meditation, yoga, support groups, massage therapy and other approaches. That number rises to approximately 90% in the cancer population. Living in the Pacific Northwest, we are fortunate to have many of these services available in the community, but until recently, patients were often on their own to locate them. Our dream was to have them available as part of the care within our oncology program and offer them at no cost to the patient. In 2011, we had a support group and a yoga class, the latter funded by an oncology nurse who saw the value in this.

At the time, there was a writing group for women who had cancer that had been started by Dr. SuEllen Pommier, a research associate at the Knight Cancer Institute who became interested in the value of writing and who was trained in the Amherst method of leading writing groups. Having a long-standing relationship, she and I began a discussion about moving the writing group into the programs offered by the Knight's Department of Patient & Family Services. We have been most fortunate to continue this offering since that time. We were very excited to add the expertise of Dawn Thompson, who has facilitated writing groups for many years, to take over the facilitation of the Women's Writing Circle. We also added Brianna Barrett who began a writing circle for adolescents and young adults who had experienced cancer. Brianna, herself a young cancer survivor, brought a particular lens on and passion about the experience, and the value of writing to express the experience. We were also fortunate to have Ryan Voelker, an employee of the Knight Cancer Institute in a different capacity and a passionate writer/facilitator, to add a Men's Writing Circle to the mix. I have periodically had the good fortune to sit in on these groups. I consistently hear, as do the facilitators, about the tremendous value of the writing circles, the healing that comes with expression through writing, and the comradery that is experienced through the safe, non-judgmental space shared with others with similar experiences.

We have been exceedingly fortunate to grow our program since that time. In addition to the one yoga and one writing group in 2012, we had a training program for massage therapists, to help the therapists learn about the unique needs of cancer patients. A few stayed on as volunteers.

With this small but important foundation, we also had a dream and a vision. Our hope was to expand our repertoire of services to include other complementary services that were truly integrated into the care of our patients. Since that time, thanks to the tireless efforts of our Foundation partners, and the generous donations from donors, we have as a permanent part of our offerings: three writing groups, yoga classes, Mindfulness-Based Stress Reduction classes, drop-in meditation sessions, support groups, and an acupuncturist/naturopath. We have been fortunate to grow the cancer massage program to offer massages to patients in the outpatient infusion clinic and the inpatient oncology units. We are especially blessed that after being furloughed during the pandemic, the massage therapists are back, much to the joy of both patients and staff members alike.

Prior to the pandemic, we offered our first Integrative Oncology Conference which showcased these resources and was offered free of charge to our patients. We hope to resume this on an annual basis.

One of the many lessons we hope to take forward post-pandemic, as the world re-groups a bit, is that many of these services can be offered online or through a virtual platform. The writing groups and support groups "pivoted" during the pandemic to a virtual meeting space. We learned that attendance was more robust, and patients reported that it was wonderful to have the option of joining these from home without the added stress of driving, parking, and navigating other issues. While online platforms are not the same as "being together" in real space and time, there are definitely advantages that we will take forward into the future.

There is no question that cancer is frightening and changes one's life in profound ways.

It is our hope that by offering supportive services that attempt to ease the fears and burdens of the cancer experience, that we are helping to heal the 'whole person.' Our writing circles are one such option.

We are exceedingly proud of the women and men who attend these groups as they navigate the cancer experience. We are indebted to and grateful for our Writing Circle Facilitators. We are thankful for the support of our donors and foundation partners.

We hope that you enjoy this anthology of writings from our participants. May you be inspired and filled with new perspectives and gratitude for life.

—Susan Hedlund, LCSW, FAOSW

Director, Patient & Family Services
Knight Cancer Institute

What Happens in a Writing Group

We sit together, in person or from the comfort of our homes. The facilitator offers up a doorway or prompt into the writing. Sometimes these doorways are an invitation to write about cancer. Other times the openings invite the writer to explore a memory, write a poem, or connect with the power of their imagination.

The writers, who often do not think of themselves as writers, allow those first words to fall onto the page. What rises up is almost always a surprise. A good surprise—whether that person is writing about something very hard or whether what comes out in the writing is irreverent or funny.

I have come to believe that within each of us dwells a wise Self or Narrator, who is always striving for our well-being and wholeness, who always knows which memory, detail, or image we need on any given day. Writing is medicine. And it is therapeutic. When we connect more deeply with ourselves and honor our experiences and our emotions, healing happens. While healing does not always mean the same thing as a cure, it does mean that which is life giving in the moment. The page helps us make sense of suffering and allows us to find meaning we may have missed. It helps us tap into our capacity for resilience, gratitude, and even joy.

After we write, we have the opportunity to share. Sharing is always optional. I remind the group that often we hesitate to share because we think what we have written is not worthwhile. "That is the best time to share," I say. "It is an act of self-love. Plus, you never know who in the circle needs to hear what you have written." And this is true. We find ourselves, our shared humanity, in one another's stories and do not feel so alone. Writing and sharing builds authentic community. In the circles, we witness through our deep listening and sometimes reflect back what we appreciate or what stays with us.

The beautiful hummingbird on the cover of this book is a symbol of the deep connections made in the circles. After participant Betsy Ames passed away in 2019, fellow writer, Marti Price Morton, who had been deeply touched by Betsy's welcoming presence in the group, felt drawn to create something for Betsy's family. She made contact, was invited over to their home and given fabric Betsy had held dear. Marti reflected, "My hope was to create a piece that the family could look at for quite some time and continue to see little parts of Betsy in. The quilt is full of Betsy's words and might be my favorite part—as if Betsy's words are still alive in the wind." Betsy's friends and family spread her ashes all over the world and when a photo of a hummingbird, which was an important animal totem to Betsy, came in from Central America, Marti knew that this was what she was meant to create. She calls the quilt *Outbreath of Beauty*, which is a line taken from poet Judith Hill's poem "Wage Peace." We are honored to share Marti's gift to Betsy's family with you.

Deb Brod, another participant, drew the flowers that grace each chapter divider, and Rick M. Cook offered his extraordinary gifts as an editor. Both of their pieces can be found in this book.

Most of the pieces you will find in this collection were not written for publication. They were written as writes that may have lasted for two minutes, eight minutes, fifteen minutes, etc. I tell writers it is amazing what can come out in two minutes. Because this is a cancer anthology, we asked participants to contribute pieces that spoke to cancer or to themes related to a life changing experience, such as grief, loss, hope, resilience, gratitude, or what promotes our well-being. The truth is we could create another anthology with all of the beautiful memoir pieces, poems, and made-up stories written each week. However, we wanted to give you, our reader, a window into the different ways life with cancer can be experienced.

We hope something in this collection touches your heart, expands your awareness and deepens your understanding and compassion of those faced with a life-changing illness. We give great thanks to Ash Good who beautifully designed and curated this book, to the writers who contributed to this anthology, to those who have participated in these groups, and to everyone at the Knight Cancer Institute at OHSU who makes these groups possible.

—Dawn Thompson, M.A.

Facilitator, Writing Group for Women Healing from Cancer
& Writing Group for Young Adults
Patient & Family Services
Knight Cancer Institute

Sometimes I think my blood comes through my pen...
Sometimes there are things that need to come out of me.
Writing makes that incision and frees my inner self...
I don't understand how anyone can live without writing.

— KELLY WALSH, 2021

a
sympathy note
to my body

Love Letter

I am only here for a short time, a moment, before I recede and all traces are swept up into mother ocean.

I walk on the shore with my dog. He is 10. He walks ahead of me, his footprints disappearing several steps behind him, filling in with sand and salt and water. In that moment of sun and surf sound, I know he will go ahead of me; a sigh of relief, but I will follow.

He does not look back at his receding footprints in the sand, so I do not look back at mine. He notices something new ahead, picks up his uneven gait and moves forward, heedless of the silent tumor in his leg.

My scarred body, I have a prayer for you, a mother's plea. Keep me as your passenger for as long as I can be contained. I will fill up your bowl with moonlight and rain, sunlight and sandy shores and loamy soil and poetry and stories. I will use your hands with intention. I will love you and tend you and I will use you to love. To mother my child. To soothe my husband. To pull my vital self from its hidden places and grow, and show, and unfold my many petals, a magnolia blossom reaching skyward before the rains come, revealing my beautiful interior until I fall apart and petals sink back to soil, sweep back to sea. ✦

Rebirth

When my mother died, I was reborn. I was five.

When I opened a notebook and discovered I could make words dance and sting, I was reborn. I was 12. It calmed the motion in my head.

When I left the wrong man for the right one, I was reborn. I was 27.

When my left nipple changed and then everything else with it—when they numbed my breast and stuck a large, hollow needle into it—I was sitting on a bench downtown the next day, my cell phone rang: cancer. I got on the bus and watched the world go by. It looked different. I was 30.

I took the poison. I cut off my breasts. I was reconstructed. It took the better part of a year. Then, every day I took the pills that shifted my hormones. I survived.

I was scarred but I healed. I went back to school. I got married. We put it behind us. I was 33.

Then my body, bulging with child, met the biopsy needle again. And the next day, again, my cell phone rang: cancer. I was 35.

We were thrown out of life and into purgatory—no way to know how far the cancer had spread until after my daughter was born. No clear course of action. But my daughter needed more time inside and if I was going to die anyway, I would give her what I could. After a surgery to remove many tumors, a nurse listened to my swollen belly with fetal monitors and told me our hearts had regained a normal rhythm, in sync.

When my daughter was born, four weeks later, cauled and crying, I was reborn. I was 35.

She was one week old, and I couldn't touch her for 24 hours after the PET scan. But it was worth it. We learned the cancer had not spread beyond my lymph nodes. It was still, technically, curable: a blessing.

She was two weeks old, and I started chemotherapy, again. An afternoon, rocking my beautiful girl, crying, sick from the treatment that kills as it saves. One thing I knew about being a mother was this: that mine had died too soon.

I took the poison—infused, ingested, irradiated. It took the better part of a year. Again, I took the pills that shifted my hormones. I survived, my daughter thrived, I thrived. We planned. I hoped for more. I was 37.

Then I went for that PET scan just to be sure. We were so sure. We wanted to be sure all was clear before another baby.

But all wasn't clear.

Again, the needle, this time in my lung, and the next day, again, my cell phone rang: cancer. It had spread. Metastatic disease. No cure.

I gasped, I grasped, I grieved, I got lost in the dark. Each day was a reckoning. I was 37.

I reached for my husband. I reached for my child. When eventually I reached for a notebook, and again I found I could make words dance and sing, I was reborn. I was 38. It calmed the motion in my head. ✦

On the Eve of My Fortieth Year

On the eve of my fortieth year as this being, I look out at the radio towers in the western hills blinking on and off in some complex rhythm I cannot follow but by now, somehow, innately know. My husband spots a shooting star—a long one, a bright one—but by the time I lift my chin and look up, it has passed. Still blazing in my husband's eyes, but, for me, the sky looks as it always has.

On the eve of my fortieth year, I wonder how many bodies I have inhabited since I was pried with forceps from my mother. Those scars have been scrubbed away by roughly passing years, but new ones seem to blossom every few years now. Will I be sad to leave this body I call home?

Even today, on the eve of my fortieth year, my body asserts her now-familiar mix of strength and weakness, fighting a summer cold but vulnerable in the first place, winning but draining my energy.

On the eve of my fortieth year, my spirit, remarkably, still yearns. Although diminished in size, scraped and sucked away by one trauma following another like elaborate floats on a demonic parade, this spirit burns brighter. As if the wear of the world and the toil of the body can sap volume but not light, so that tonight, on the eve of my fortieth year, I am already the brightest star in the night sky. ✦

ELENA WIESENTHAL is a mother, writer, and nonprofit consultant living in Portland, Oregon. She loves getting lost in a good book, walking the beaches of the coasts and old growth forests of Oregon, cooking and eating and traveling, and snuggling with her daughter, dog, and husband. Elena was first diagnosed with breast cancer in 2005 and has been living with metastatic illness since 2014. Writing helps her heal and process life's uncertainties, sorrows, and joys.

Scanxiety

Scanxiety. Every time. My next PET scan is on Monday, and it's pretty much all I can think about. I met my new oncologist last week. I like her, but she's pretty blunt. She said I was at high risk for recurrence. Wait, what?? My previous oncologist said recurrence was "definitely a concern," but in my book that's not the same as "high risk." How high risk are we talking? Can I get a statistic? It had me slightly worried.

And then I went and did something completely and totally stupid. I knew better, but I did it anyway. I googled "Ewing Sarcoma recurrence."

*F**k!*

Pardon my language, but there's nothing else that does this feeling justice. Apparently, best case scenario is a 15% five-year survival rate if this thing comes back. If it comes back with distant metastases like it did before . . . 0.9%. I've just been told I'm at high risk for almost definitely being dead within five years.

I've got my follow-up in one week and one day. After that I can stop fearing for my life and laugh at how silly I was being. For the next 182 hours though, I'll continue to freak the F out! ☏

Scars

In the summer, I like to wear low cut tank tops that show my port-a-cath scar. I have some survivor friends that hide their scars. One has a barely noticeable line on her neck from thyroid surgery and almost never leaves the house without a scarf. I have a really hard time understanding this.

We survived cancer! That is badass! Why would anyone want to hide such a triumph?

My scar is my medal of valor. Sometimes I almost wish it looked more impressive, as selfish as it sounds. Yes, there were rough days. Yes, there was pain. But I got through it. And if I can get through that, I can get through anything.

My scar is a constant encouragement that makes me smile every time I see it. ❧

JULIANA PERSON spends her working hours as a winery lab manager and her nonworking hours as a storyteller, outdoor enthusiast, intrepid traveler, and voracious reader of Harry Potter fanfiction. She moved to Oregon in 2015 shortly after finishing treatment for Ewing sarcoma and has been a regular attendee of the OHSU Writing Group for Young Adults Healing from Cancer ever since.

Heart

After my mastectomies, I came home raw and weary. I couldn't shower for a few days, and when I finally did, I needed my husband's help undressing. I stood as he unpeeled me in front of the mirror—first my bathrobe, then my bandages—and braced myself for the big reveal. The body staring back at me was battered, misshapen, and startlingly purple, but there was also a sweet surprise: a bright blue heart colored onto my chest, a few inches under my collarbone.

The heart seemed to be drawn in permanent marker and was about the size of an Oreo. It was the kind of heart I like to make—perfectly symmetrical, with two chubby sides. Imagining a doctor or nurse taking time to draw this heart in the midst of my surgery made my chest fill with warmth and my eyes flood with tears. It seemed like a sympathy note to my body, written on my body, and an honoring of my own grieving heart. In that most vulnerable moment, it felt like the kindest thing in the world.

Later, I would realize the heart was on my right side, above the breast that had cancer. I would wonder if the heart was just some O.R. shorthand. I would wonder: did the heart mean "cancer" or did the heart mean "love?" But there in front of the mirror, I just stood and stared a little longer, taking everything in. ✤

How are the New Boobs?

Lately everyone's been asking how I like my new boobs, as if they were a crazy mid-life splurge, or the rice cooker they've been eyeing at Costco. I find this, like so many questions of the past six months, nearly impossible to answer. I know what they want to hear:

They're amazing!

Perky!

Major cancer bonus: Free boob job!

Highly recommend.

But here's what I want to say:

They are uncomfortable. They feel odd, foreign, and numb. I notice them all the time. They look okay when I'm dressed or standing, but when I bend over, they ripple across the top. When I take my bra off, they are temporarily misshapen. There's one dent that never evens out. It reminds me of an avocado that was tested for ripeness with one very big thumb. They are cold to the touch, which often creeps me out. When I hold them in my hands, I can feel the clumps of fat that were donated by my own thighs. When I think about the hidden "cadaver mesh," I wonder who's in there, holding me up. When they're not constantly reminding me of cancer or the natural body I used to have, they're just about perfect.

So that's how I'm enjoying the new boobs. Thanks for asking! ✠

Surrender

I am not done with my changes. I'm in the hardest time—the sorting, the figuring-it-all-out. It's comforting to think I might not have to will this so much, effort this so much. I try so hard to make it all happen, to control my course, but maybe I need to trust in a greater process at work. How do I surrender? I fear I won't get it right, that I won't make the changes I most need to make. I want to look back on this moment as a turning point, see how everything lined up after now, after then, how it all makes perfect sense in hindsight, how I lived well. I want to live well.

There are spontaneous changes, like how I ran into the surf this weekend, the cold ocean washing over me, licking my legs with its icy tongues while I laughed above it, joy rippling through my body as I ran up the beach and into the hot tub. That would never have happened before. Nor would I have insisted on naked hot tubbing before. Life's too short for bathing suits in the hot tub. Silliness. Play. Maybe this is my surrender. ✦

HILLARY H. is a one-year breast cancer survivor. Writing in community has been her best medicine. She lives in Portland with her family and one very curly dog.

Metamorphosis

Endless, boundless energy; my lifelong companion. From youth until cancer chemo treatments started at age 65, I had really only known myself through my physical energy and well-being.

Soccer teams, trail running through forests, dance classes, swimming, bike riding everywhere, yoga, skiing, hiking . . . I could go on and on.

For forty years, my morning routine was up at 5:00 am, a cup of coffee, then straight out for a morning run. Usually a hilly, five-mile run before work. At lunch, I'd grab an aerobics class before rushing back to my desk. After work was an ecstatic dance session, then a long ride through Forest Park back home.

Up until my cancer chemo started, I couldn't imagine not exercising four to five hours a day. I couldn't fathom staying in bed beyond 5:30 am. It wasn't within the realm of possibility that I wouldn't be out climbing hills and leaping down. I was an endorphin junkie and no doubt about it.

Then I began chemo. My type of breast cancer was triple positive. It demanded 12 weeks of three-hour infusions with drugs so toxic that the nurses wrapped themselves in plastic, protective gear as they connected tubes and began the scary drips. Wavering between hope and fear, the drugs which killed cells indiscriminately, dripped into my stilled body for hours.

I fought the fatigue until I couldn't. All at once I had to accept the reality that my energy was ebbing away. No longer did I leave my bed early to run in any weather. At some point, I faced up to the fact that I hadn't left my bed for three days.

My knowledge of myself evaporated. I did not know who I was without an energy, which now seemed almost like a slavedriver.

After the mastectomy and reconstruction surgeries, the chemo treatment became less often and less toxic.

Little sprouts of energy began to bud. However, this time I felt I now deserved to also have the right to rest. Now, as the chemo is nearing its end, I feel a new, more peaceful desire to exercise and move my body.

The fatigue that once devastated me has become a teacher. Instead of the slave-driving component to my former boundless energy, I've discovered a more gentle, nurturing energy. I feel this new energy is like a new friend, one that I look forward to getting to know. ✦

Bliss is Always within Reach!

I am acutely aware of shallow versus deep breathing. I have long studied breathwork as an essential and beloved part of my yoga journey.

As the result of this study, breath has filled me with unity, joy, and energy which is well described by the word *ecstasy*.

When my breath turns shallow, I realize I'm rejecting my ability to empower my own connection to feeling better. I cling to the shallow in breath and out breath as a way to stay miserable.

I vigorously shake. I long to break through and fill my entire being with oxygen from the pure air.

Sometimes, if I try hard enough, this longing reaches such an intensity that I actually do it! Deep, soothing, beloved breaths. ❦

SONA JOINER is a life-long seeker and hoper, ready to begin the third act of her life. Gratitude is her only attitude.

The Burn

Scott and Andrya are my radiation techs. Blessed I am to have them be my angels of mercy during my therapies. Every day for the last 21 days, I have the honor of being greeted by these two caring individuals. They fetch me from a small waiting room, just for us radiation patients and always request a warm blankie. We go into the treatment room where I lie on the designated table, and, as they position me, we chat. They dial in the songbird track for my listening therapy, and when ready, they disappear and I am treated.

These are very special people . . . not because of what they do, but how they choose to do it. With care. They share their personalities and private lives. I feel like I'm visiting friends every morning.

Here's an example of Scott's bedside manner: I see my radiologist after my treatment every Wednesday. I am wearing a gown with an open back. The room I await my doctor in is chilly. Scott comes in and drapes a warm blanket around my shoulders to warm me. This also warms my heart.

Andrya and I have a fondness for birds. She just received several books on birdwatching. This is *her* therapy. She knows how I desire to hear those chirps and songs during my treatments so she does an intentional search on Pandora, and today on YouTube, to find the most therapeutic listening possible.

We chat about our dogs, the virus, our families, and guess what, time goes so quickly I wish I could spend more time with them. Yes, I will reach out. Perhaps we will see one another after the pandemic is over. I've already told them how much I'll miss them. They laugh this off of course, as it is bittersweet. Notes from my heart and some sweet things from the bakery tomorrow is the least I can provide. They need to know how important they are to their patients, to me. ✦

Radiation Routine

Many have asked just what happens when you announce that you're going through radiation treatments. Here's a synopsis of my last five days . . .

Upon the first visit, you get tattooed, three dots on the torso so that the machine will align itself to your body and have perfect aim. Painful? A "2" on the 1–10 pain scale. Other things that are beyond the layman's mental capacity happen. The time lapsed is an hour or so.

The daily routine for the next 23 days:

Check-in at the front desk, go to a dressing room, strip from waist up, wait in a small room just for us radiation patients. The tech fetches you and brings you into the place where it all happens and asks about your choice of music (they pump in music to relax you). You then lie upon a narrow table that has a beam of light running down the center, a movable hard barrier that is placed just beneath your butt (to ensure you aren't going to move), a wedge under your knees for comfort. They place your arms above your head that rest in placers so they don't have movement. If you wish a warm blankie (who doesn't?), they lay that on your legs. Your head is turned to the left and must stay there. Next, for me, since I have a defibrillator, they place a piece of lead to defend my body against the rays (usually taped to my body), then they dial in the machine. Once they have your body dialed in, you may not move.

The device is large. It is cold, mean looking, and makes some weird noise when operating, which I've labeled hissing. The techs leave you alone. You are on camera. They have recording devices so if you are in distress, they can hear. The hissing starts (the angle is 9 o'clock), then stops, then starts, then stops. The machine then whirls overhead and stops around 4 o'clock. The same thing happens. This is a very sobering experience. It's just like birth and death. It's just you, so there's time to reflect, and for me, I choose to channel friends and family members that are deceased.

On my first treatment, I asked them to play soothing classical music. "Clare de Lune" starts, and I know that my mother is holding me close, since she requested I play that on the piano when I was a child. Since then, I choose to channel others that bring forth memories and comfort while the hissing begins, then subsides. I am trying to make peace with the beast of the machine, but it pays me no mind, as it has a job to do.

The timeline in the actual radiation is a matter of eight minutes, prep is longer. You are in and out in a matter of a half hour. The staff is professional and have the best bedside manners. I've been told that the treatment does not compromise the immune system, which is pretty important considering what's happening in our world.

My side effects: I am not as mentally sharp, seem to have a haze around me. Fatigue is slowly setting in; my skin is holding up with special creams and oils applied twice a day. The tenth treatment is when redness may set in with some discomfort. At present, I'm doing well, a bit lethargic, trying my best to get my "to do list" done.

They will do a "boost" treatment (last five) in which they will aim a direct hit to the area where my tumor lived. Presently they trigger a larger area that runs from armpit to center of torso to sternum. They drew a circle on my body so that I could see where I should apply creams. I was surprised to see how large it was.

That's my little routine that I will follow five days a week, through April 14th. Not so bad. At least there is no chemo this time, and since it's my second time around, there are no surprises (at least I pray not).

I pray for the world and its creatures, and hope that we all open our eyes to just how precious life is, as is our planet. ✔

The Guide's Silhouette

Fatigue called my name
Treatments had flushed me of all energy
I lie in bed
Facing four windows
Seeing a chimney, tree tops
It is raining
Sounds of drops gurgling
Teasing the rain gutters
Dancing on leaves
Splashing in puddles
Cables attached to our home
Stretched inches from my window
A bird's silhouette
Finding recluse from the wet
There it sat
Sometimes one leg attached
Sometimes both
I would doze in and out of slumber
Awakening, it would still be there
My wondrous feathered spirit guide
Looking after me
Reassuring all would be ok
And it was
For that moment of solace and comfort
Gratitude ✦

DENISE SIRCHIE is a three-time cancer survivor. One of Denise's missions in life is to assist in the healing process of others. Whether this be through her writing, hands-on help, or creating mosaic art, it rewards her as she reflects on the people she has helped battling their demons. Strangers, as well as family and friends, whisper their needs. She hears, then implements that which life has intended.

Post-Surgery

I heal and recover

my itchy red scabs

turn to rough purple scars

and my rough purple scars

will turn to smooth lines

that tell a story.

The story of how

my itchy red scabs

that became rough purple scars

were once wounds

held together with stitches

from surgery to remove

my tumor and bone.

The story of how

I heal and recover. ✦

My 21st Birthday

In the same week of my 21st birthday, I developed a cocktail recipe that only a 21-year-old cancer patient would ever think to make: a drink that tastes like Nystatin. During treatment, I had several neutropenic fevers and as a result, I was on antibiotics a lot which caused me to develop oral thrush a couple of times. Nystatin is an anti-fungal mouthwash that is cherry-peppermint flavored. It seems like an odd and unpleasant flavor combination, but it actually doesn't taste too bad. To make this drink, just mix three parts half and half, two parts cherry vodka, and one part peppermint schnapps. The cream will curdle a little, but that just makes it a similar consistency to Nystatin that isn't shaken prior to use. To drink and get the full Nystatin experience: take a sip, swish it around your mouth, hold the drink in your mouth for a bit, and then swallow.

That week I also completed chemotherapy. Both are milestones that felt forever away when I was first diagnosed with Ewing sarcoma. The celebrations kicked off at 13K while I was still receiving chemo when the wonderful nurses gifted me a slice of cake and a thoughtful card. The day of my birthday, I celebrated at my local infusion clinic with a blood draw and subsequently learned that I needed transfusions of blood and platelets. So, I was given blood products for my birthday—blood is definitely one of the best gifts people can give. The following day, I had a small birthday party with the OHSU Young Adult Cancer Writing Group. Not quite a typical 21st birthday party, but it was so great to celebrate my birthday with writing games and with people who supported and mentored me through treatment. ✔

CARALYNN HAMPSON is a college student and Ewing sarcoma survivor. Caralynn is majoring in biostatistics, theology, and religious studies and loves playing with LEGOs, reading, and cuddling with cats.

Resilience

Resilience is made up of half memory and half amnesia.

I'd dreaded the days I had to get my treatment in the hospital.

The smell of the infusion room was something that I became infinitely familiar with. It was a composite of plastic IV bags and vinyl upholstery with the aura of disinfectant solution on sturdy metallic furniture. The air had hints of every person's clothing and their body, their breath, and perfumes.

I could already start to smell this on my way over in the car. It is stitched into my memory of the infusion room. It was attached to my dread of the side effects of my chemotherapy.

After I took my seat to begin the injection, I felt like a part of the room—I blended into the smells of the space and the furniture. The saline liquid was how they began the process, so I smelled how that entered my body, and by then, the main medicines followed steadily and proportionately just up to the threshold of what my body could take. I would drift off mentally, but I could feel everything. My cells were dying, and my blood count was declining as planned.

After I got home, the smells would stay with me somewhat. But the layers lifted away as I recovered and my counts increased, my nausea faded, and my body strengthened. The smell, the memories, and the symptoms peeled away. I'd forget that dreaded confluence—and I felt better again as if nothing had happened. ✸

Everywhere Else

Lying in bed, my eyes wandered. They were straining, but curious. Perhaps my eyes strained because of the wondering. But it was hard to focus on one thing at the time. Too much was happening in the isolation ward I was staying in.

I looked at things in the way a scanner copies an image. I tried to keep everything—see everything—even though not much was actually happening. The way I was positioned, with my head on the pillow elevated, I felt I was expected to see everything. The nurse had forgotten to write her name on the board. The bathroom door was left slightly ajar so I could peek inside. My urinal was close by. The photos of my family were up by the door. I could see a leftover glove on the floor that was clean but had to be thrown away.

Now was the time. I had to stay completely still for the nurse to remove my port, but it was hard. The more I remained still, the easier it would be for them. But it wasn't so easy. The port had grown accustomed to my chest. The skin had healed over it and accepted it, so removal was painful and bloody. To make sure I didn't squirm around, I focused my attention everywhere else in that room and scanned across to look at everything except myself. ✦

ALPEN SHETH works in technology and social impact and lives in Miami with his wife, daughter, and dog. He has had two stem-cell transplant treatments for Hodgkin's Lymphoma. Alpen has written with the Writing Group for Young Adults Healing from Cancer.

Grandpa Alva—How He Died

The coroner eyed the cases of Bacardi rum in the back bedroom in Portland, Oregon, where my grandpa died. I think he died of some kind of bone cancer. I'm not sure what was officially listed as the cause of death though. He was a fine carpenter who repaired antique furniture, lived to almost 80, always had a cigar nearby, and was a lifelong alcoholic. Until we got older, my siblings and I were a little afraid of him. His wife, my grandma, who never smoked or drank, died at 63 from liver cancer. After she died, he became a recluse and lived in an A-frame cabin near the Umpqua river in southern Oregon, mining for gold. He drove an old Packard Woody from the 1940s. Once I saw that he kept a picture I made for them when I was small, taped up in that old wagon. It surprised me that he loved me.

I visited him in the hospital and asked, "How are you doing?"

He said, while coughing fiercely and gasping for breath, "I'd like to know how the hell I got mixed up with this operation," referring to his experience of the overall functioning and daily routines of the hospital. I also sensed he was referencing a military operation, perhaps harkening back to his days as a soldier in WWI. He never had a surgical operation. He never took any of the pain medication sent home with him to my mother's house from the hospital. My grandpa had his own way of dealing with pain. Looking at his body after he died, it seemed so clear that he wasn't there.

Some people linger in a way, but Alva, I think, was eager to get back to the hills and river. He'd come down briefly only to leave his body. ❧

Hearing The News

The womb is a noisy place; incessant drumming of hearts beating in their rhythms, the swishing, slurping, whining of nearby bowels, mysterious sounds of breath and voice. When I was young, I liked to ask my mother about my birth. She always gave me vague answers. Later I realized she was in twilight, the condition induced by drugs to anesthetize women for childbirth, given in the early to mid-twentieth century. In the womb, I listened in a particular way to the essence of our sounds, felt the vibration of our liquids shaking developing organs and the makings of skin. We don't hear only with our ears; we hear with what forms our heart, too.

Above all else, I loved the sound of my mother's voice. The closest I can come to describing the sound of her voice there in the womb, is hearing the voice of god. Afterwards it was different, the voice changed. She now had four children to care for. I felt urgent need. She had to let me cry. And cry I did. Was this the same mother?

Cancer and all its words are cacophonous. It is something that can kill me. Though something could kill me faster—another person, a car, a heart attack, a stroke, a different kind of cancer, a bear. When I heard, "You have cancer," it sounded like an alarm. I panicked and I tried to hide it. I was afraid.

However, after a while, "You have cancer" started to sound like a long, slow release message. "Cancer" sounded like a loud, deep, resonant, trailing gong—wake up, be serious, be whimsical, feel all the sorrows and all the love, be afraid, be powerful, say "help," know all is well.

I remembered how to listen the way I did before I had ears. ✦

SUSAN GLADSTONE lives in Portland, Oregon, with her husband, Alan. She participates regularly in the women's writing circle sponsored by the Knight Cancer Institute at OHSU. Walking in a city, near a river, or in the forest is a favorite pastime.

Breathless

On the very same day I heard I had lymphoma, I also volunteered for the first time in Lyla's Pre-K class at PJA. I arrived and she bounded out of her chair and into my arms hugging me so tightly she took my breath away. Minutes before as I drove to her school, my doctor called me to confirm his diagnosis of lymphoma and that took my breath away, too.

How is it possible to make room for so much breathlessness all in one day, one hour, one car ride? And, overall, it was a lovely day.

Next, I went to Leo's school, Ainsworth, where I volunteer every week. He was having a tough day and asked me to take him home. Here I am, a recently diagnosed lymphoma patient, my nana's heart strings pulled by a seven-year-old.

"Take me home," he begs.

"Leave him here," his teacher urges. "He'll be fine. I think it's just nerves."

I have no nerves for telling him *no*—I am a nana with lymphoma. I never say *no* to you, sweet Leo.

Lyla bounds into my arms. You both bound into my heart.

I prefer to well my woes with both of you. ❧

Cancer Ward

OSHU, Building #2. Enter the underground parking garage and search for a parking space. Around and around, I drive, finding those spaces closest to a wall divider into which I can never maneuver my car. So, on I go, around and around till finally, I find a space. Then I must locate the elevator for Building 2, not Building 1. I've made that mistake before and ended up more disoriented than usual.

There is a disorientation associated with this whole experience of entering the cancer ward. My heart races, my mind boggles, fear has its way with me. I finally arrive in Building 2 and find the other bank of elevators that take me up. I haven't been in Building 2 since COVID closed our in-person writing group last year. But here I am, same place, same feelings, arriving to meet my new oncologist, Dr. Spurgeon. First stop, the lab for bloodwork.

I stand in line, six feet away from my nearest neighbor, then check-in, new insurance, new patient, same old questions, but how did she know about my new insurance—I feel happy about that and alarmed—how does this information spread? Then into the lab, one jab, two vials of red liquid, one BAND-AID, and back to the elevator to floor 10. Check-in is easy, directed to seating area 5.

I walk past a man I'd seen in the lab area. He has his mask off so he can eat a cookie and drink a juice box. I sit as far away from him as I can. I think annoying, angry thoughts about him and feel tempted to tell him to go outside to eat and to keep his mask on in here. I don't.

Then I look at him more closely, so thin, so frail, so unkempt. He's not here for fun or games or laughs. My heart softens slightly, but still the fear permeates my being. Fear distances me from my compassionate side, and I remind myself to honor all those essential workers who put their safety on the line daily to help others. I say a small prayer for my frail waiting room companion as he is called into his/our oncologist's office. *May we both be safe, healthy, and surrounded by kindness.*

Perhaps I'm not always as open-hearted as I fancy myself. ⊀

BONNIE FOLICK fully retired from her career in social work/therapy in 2011. She and her husband, Josh, relocated from Ashland to Milwaukie, Oregon, in 2014 to be closer to their three sons, daughters-in-law, and grandchildren. Bonnie enjoys gardening, fiber arts, biking, hiking, reading, writing, and perfecting the art of grandparenting.

HANNAH KIMBERLY

Cadillac of Cancers

"It's the Cadillac of cancers."

That's funny, I don't remember ordering a Cadillac. The oncologist didn't say anything about luxury car care at my appointment. If it's a Cadillac, can I take it back? I'd rather not have it actually. The reality is, Cadillac or lemon, the kind of cancer you want is no cancer. I'm grateful for people I've met and lessons I've learned along the way. I try not to hold on to anger, and I take the situation for what it is. But if I could snap my fingers and have never had cancer, I absolutely would.

People think they are being reassuring. They think it's comforting to tell you, "it's the *good* cancer." People don't really know how to talk about cancer most of the time. I fully understand that, but it still makes statements like that incredibly invalidating, although some of them are funny to laugh about later. I often feel like I'm in some middle ground. People outside the cancer world may think of me as unlucky, that I drew the short straw. But in the cancer world—I see sicker people often. I have lost friends and family to cancer. I am fully aware of the very harsh realities of this disease. And I recognize how "lucky" I am.

The guilt that comes with a more treatable cancer haunts me already. I don't need to hear more reminders of how great you think I have it. Sometimes I struggle to find the balance between holding space for my situation being tough and acknowledging it could be so much worse. Yes, I've had Stage 3 cancer twice, but I've had options in my treatment and my recent scans have looked good. Often, it's hard to talk about my situation in a raw way. I usually end up filtering what I'm saying depending on the setting, which results in me minimizing things or putting a positive spin on everything.

Cancer is isolating enough without worrying that I am taking up too much space. ✦

Superficial Armor

Is it shallow to say I feel more like myself than I have in years now that my hair is lighter and thicker again? The first time I went through treatment, I shaved my head rather than let it fall out because that was a small way that I could take control at a time when there was so much out of my control. It was a painfully slow process for my hair to grow back. I wore wigs over my awkward hair growth as I waited for it to be more than thin wisps on my head. I never told my clients I had cancer so I bought a wig that was as close to my real hair as possible. Wigs were my protection as I tried to cling to some semblance of normal. Finally, my hair grew out enough I could take the wigs off at work. I smiled through all the compliments from clients about my cute new haircut while I was cringing on the inside, hating that I had a constant external reminder of what I went through.

My hair was finally to my shoulders and was a semblance of my past self when my oncologist confirmed that my cancer was back. This time around, I did not lose my hair, but it did thin out significantly. I've kept my hair short while I waited for the layers to come back. And they slowly have.

Last month I got highlights and a trim and felt pretty again. It's really hard to admit how big of a difference it makes to have hair that feels like me again. It brings me closer to that ever-elusive feeling of who I was before. As much as I know I will never be that person again, it is nice to have some of the superficial armor back. It makes it easier to pretend momentarily that so much hasn't changed. It brings back some of my old confidence for a bit. Having some control over my appearance feels empowering on many levels. I've accepted that even if it's a silly thing to put so much value in, it's a small thing that makes me happy, and I'll always be grateful for small things that make me happy. ⸙

Visiting You

I'm at a place
That's not how I want it to be
I hoped for a quiet night here
But we pull up to the park and it's free symphony night
We have to park down the block and there's way too many people
It's so loud and distracting
We walk over to see your tree
It's my first time I've been back since your tree was added
There's a whole grove of trees like this one
The trees all look similar, identical plaques in front of them
With different names and details
I want to feel a sense of peace
Or connection
But I mostly just feel sadness
And guilt, the guilt is always there
The people at the next tree over are shouting and laughing
As I stand there with tears in my eyes
I'm grateful I can come to this place
To see a part of her here
I don't need to come to a park to remember my friend
Or to feel close to her
But still—it's nice to have a physical place to come to

I walk around the pond afterwards
Wondering, asking, demanding why

Why there were such different outcomes for two girls who got different
types of blood cancer
There are no answers to be found
It's not fair—of course, it's not
None of this is.

I think of all the places she wanted to go
The things she never got to do
Having a job after college, dealing with a boring Monday at work
And she won't get to
But here I am
Here I am.
Survivor's guilt and grief twisted together so tightly
It's impossible to say where one ends and the other begins
I miss my friend
And I'm glad I could come see her in this place
This park with too many people
The sounds of summer, the music drifting
It's not perfect but it feels real ❦

HANNAH KIMBERLY has participated in the Writing Group for Young Adults
Healing from Cancer for three years and is grateful for the chance to connect with
the cancer community in this way. She is currently going through treatment for
Hodgkin's Lymphoma for the second time.

I Am

I am made of loops of time
Of first breaths and lasts
Of sun casting sideways, kissing my feet in the room I was born 33 years later
On the last month I was whole
I am born

New blood in my veins
And with it, unexpected years
Wrapped in skin that trembles
And exchanges scars with the bark of trees older than civilization
I am unexpected
I am

I am here
I am blessed with toes that become time travelers when they press into
cool cut grass, and I am again that summer child
Stepping from the sloshing kiddie pool in the lawn,
just before her first bee sting

I am free of future
I am in the loop, in the know,
I've seen behind the curtain
We've all been traveling backward since the beginning

I am expected
I am blessed with gratitude
As I carry my oxygen sloped across my back, metal clapping at my hip
Through crowds who take their breathing for granted

I am here
And even my sleep feels like living
And bones in sand
If I rest
I am aware
Aware
Of how much dancing I will be doing ❦

Backpack

I ordered a backpack once.
Great deal,
Lost in a discount outdoor website

Small, tan, perfect for what I needed . . . Which wasn't much
And when it came
Wrapped in its shroud of plastic and shipping labels,
Only then did I realize it was meant for a child
No reference to size in the photos

And I hold it now sometimes
And wonder if I could have known its utility
The size of a notebook
A laptop if its hungry
Sunglasses, pens, and painkillers zipped snuggly in that front pocket

Wouldn't have known it then,
When I slammed it into the sand at the beach
On a surf day stolen from mid-week
When I saw it had potential to hold cider and sunscreen

That its small size, only a few years later, would be its great strength
As my own strength dwindled
Sliding it gently from shoulder to shoulder in hospital hallways

Masks,
and always a backup
A yellow legal pad
Notes, numbers, names, diagnosis,
Pen scratched efforts of "keeping it together"

Emesis bags and a planner full of appointments
Too many appointments

But sometimes,
While I wait,
Sometimes
I slip open its edges,
And still smell sand ✦

Pictures

And here we crash,
softly,
on the boardwalk in the high desert.
A brief rip in sky creates some sun-caked hallway
The day has hardly begun and we've cried,
been angry,
held each other
tightly, talking about death and dreams
A normal Monday, you might say
While I wait for you to join me,
Here

Instead, you pull out your phone to take a picture
And all I can think is
I wish I had a different face,
The one I used to carry.
But I smile, because these pictures are for you
For after I'm gone
And I am not one to judge
What face you want to remember ❧

LENA TRAENKENSCHUH was born on a hill just outside of Port Townsend, Washington, under the fiery boughs of a madrona tree, but now calls Portland, Oregon, her home. She danced before she could walk, and for a time it was her career, working collaboratively, founding a dance collective, creating dance films, and performing internationally. Though leukemia and a bone marrow transplant became more than just a minor bump in the road, she feels lucky she can spend more time than ever reuniting with one of her first passions, a love of the outdoors. Writing has become a great comfort in the middle of some great years of change, but she feels most grateful for the connection with others it has fostered. She believes there may be nothing more healing than to tell your story and receive the gift of someone else's story in return.

Cancer Scars

Four inches. That's the incision's length the thoracic surgeon made in my back. Four inches and God knows what other lacerations he made to the muscles under my left scapula. Four inches that allowed a mechanical spreader to hold other muscles out of the way so he could get to the chest wall and make another incision to remove the rib cage tissues for my lymphoma biopsy. It would be many months later that we learned a critical nerve in my back had been damaged during that surgery, damage that would cause me daily pain for the rest of my life. Still, every day above ground is a good day.

There's yet another scar on this body of mine. Unseen but felt all the same. Deep and aching, the one in my rib cage radiates throughout my body, keeping me up at night with time to think while waiting for the Oxycodone to take effect.

Thinking. Thinking about my life. About how lucky I am to have the wonderful, supportive wife I have. I married her, nine years my senior, thinking that we'll both age together well, that given how much longer women outlive their husbands, that nine years ought to be just right for when we approach that final bridge. We may cross it closer together, one not having to live much longer without the other when whoever should pass first. But now, looking ahead, is that road forking?

Why do I think of these things? It's the cancer scare, again. A scar seemingly etched on my brain permanently. I'll never know that I'm free of cancer forever. Never. But I hope to look back at ninety years of age and thumb my nose at this ever-lurking monster of the shadows.

Until then, I'll be happy to never have another surgery, never gain another scar. One badge of courage is enough for me. Though I can't see it, I can feel it like a gremlin on my back, as well as the one in my brain, always threatening my positive thoughts and aspirations with the melancholic muck of doubt and despair.

Acupuncture doesn't help, and massage only yields temporary relief. Four inches that will go down as a battle scar in this civil war. Daily, it reminds me to live life to its fullest, to be thankful for each waking moment, while my mental battle rages on. ✸

Cancer and Superstition

I've never really had much "faith" in superstition, not after getting over the fact that my mama's back was just fine no matter how many cracks I'd stepped on along the way home from school. I was broken of that brain pattern of fear when a friend derided me for hopping & skipping to avoid sidewalk cracks when I thought I wasn't being observed. He made fun of me, belittling me, but fortunately not in front of others. Still, it was enough to make me realize that you don't have to believe everything anyone tells you and, more importantly, to face your fears.

Stepping back from it now, I put a positive spin on all things superstitious and either make fun of them or try to understand the roots of those malformed brain patterns. Why do people believe the crazy things they do? Why is Friday the 13th a day of bad luck? With a positive spin, it usually turns out to be a great day because I'm consciously focusing on it being just that. So why can't we focus on the positive, drop the negative, and live in a better world, one full of stronger hopes, dreams, aspirations, and good feelings?

That's the way I tackled cancer, by thinking positively as often as I can. I'm not always successful. Even after the lymphoma came back for an encore presentation (and leukemia after that!), I kept my faith in science and OHSU's brilliant oncologists. I bombarded those bad, superstitious thoughts with a counterattack of good ones. Still, the inevitable questions gnawed at me. Did I catch lymphoma by breathing it in from my friend who died of it three months prior? Was my diet to blame? Is God punishing me and for what? And the most damaging of all: Why is my body attacking me?

Who cares? At this point, it was simply a matter of survival. I couldn't change the past, but I *could* choose how to face this adversity, and possibly even death if it came to that. I knew if I gave up, there would be little hope of surviving this disease, an illness, by the way, that would've been a death sentence thirty years ago. I was fortunate to have these doctors and nurses saving my life. I could at least do my part.

A strong mind leads to a strong body. And superstition has no place in either. ✦

Thrice in a Lifetime

People have asked me, "Well, how did you get here?"

Not to sound too much like a Talking Heads song, but it's amazing how far and how fast I've progressed down this road of battling lymphoma (twice, now). The shock is still wearing off. On December 30, 2009, I was only forty-eight. This sort of stuff wasn't supposed to happen to me for another thirty years! And being from Louisiana, I thought good old-fashioned heart disease from all the rich, fried Cajun food would do me in, long before cancer ever had a chance to show its dastardly face. Not so, apparently.

The problems started perhaps as early as 2008. It's so hard to tell because the docs don't know exactly what causes lymphoma nor how long the buildup was to the actual manifestation of symptoms. In any case, I didn't feel anything prior to Halloween 2009, when I was *trying* to do sit-ups in my hotel room while on a business trip. The pain felt like I'd ripped an abdominal muscle. During winter, it grew to the point I could no longer sleep on my back or left side. Turns out it was some enlarged abdominal lymph nodes pressing down on my spine and lungs, causing mild leg paralysis and breathing difficulties.

I'll never forget December 22nd or the dour look on the radiologist's face or his words when he came back with my CT scan results. "Go to your GP. Today. Right now. He's waiting for you."

Blindsided, I somehow made it to the car and called my wife. I couldn't speak for twenty seconds before finally muttering, "They found something." We both cried then, for a very long time.

A diagnosis of lymphoma must take the cake for the Crummiest Christmas Present Ever. And I couldn't even take it back on Boxing

Day! Lucky me. I had half a mind to talk to Santa about this one. I mean, c'mon, Old Man. Has inflation gone up so much that a lump of coal just doesn't cut it anymore?

That's where it began for me. And it's been a long struggle ever since. Thankfully, an incredible oncology team at OHSU steered my lymphoma into remission in 2013 using my own stem cells. But now, leukemia has risen to take its place. I continue to soldier on. Two down, one to go! ✔

RICK M. COOK is a three-time survivor of cancer, having battled lymphoma twice, and is currently thrashing leukemia's butt. The OHSU Writing Group for Men Healing from Cancer rekindled his childhood desire to publish short stories. Since his three-week isolation in OHSU's 14K "Bone Marrow Transplant Unit" in 2013, he has published three short stories in two anthologies and is currently working on his debut sci-fi novel. You can find him at: https://linktr.ee/RickMCook.

into the
dark forest

Welcome to Canceristan

Welcome to Canceristan: leave your I.D. at the door. Your passport to the country of cancer is a diagnosis or the diagnosis of a loved one. You are either cared for or caregiver here. I'd say caretaker, but oddly caregiver and caretaker are the same thing. Either way, it's a give with far too much take. And far too much at stake.

There is a stripping process. Your clothes. Your jewelry—your watch and sense of time. You will be asked to leave your familiar, comfortable places. You will be given an armband. You will be expected to be patient. In fact, this is your new name here: Patient. An unfunny irony. One of the many to come.

This place is disorienting. People who are not from here are full of advice. They imagine they know what it's like and what you will need. But really, there is no way to know how to become a refugee. This is not something that can be taught. This is not something anyone aspired to.

In the beginning, there is boot camp. It is harsh. Some don't survive.

Even when you go back home, after this, to your comfortable familiar, you will feel, still, the nagging sense that you are living in exile. Such is the power of cancer and its reach. Once a citizen here, always a citizen. A passport impossible to revoke no matter how much you may want to give it up.

Who you were before entry here matters little. You have a new uniform here. A new buzz cut. You are a soldier-survivor now. Whether you like this identity or not.

You will get to know the others who work here. Aid workers and mercenaries. You will recognize them by their uniforms. And resent their ability to be airlifted home at any time.

The economy here is convoluted and contradictory. So many warring factions. And there is too much war terminology here.

To come to know and be watchful of the threat indicators, you learn to live in a state of panic, become normalized to the tang in the back of the throat, the fine hairs standing up on the backs of wrists and neck.

You may not ever get good at this, if such a thing is possible.

What becomes hard is the ability to foresee a future beyond this place, this permanently temporary way of life. The past will become saturated in elegy. The future murky and too frightening to consider.

You've seen the signs. Counted the dead. The death toll rises. Politicians prognosticate, prevaricate. But you: you just survive. It's what each day brings now. Another thing to look away from, another thing to resist considering.

This is you now. This is your home.

Welcome to Canceristan. Leave your I.D. at the border. May all who enter here be blessed. May they know peace one day. ❤

On Hope

"Forget your hope," reads one translation of the hell gate inscription in Dante's *Inferno*.

There is so much talk of hope in Cancerland. The people who stand outside, the people who stand beside and bedside of us, willingly take on blind hope. They step into it like a band of light and surrender all darkness to it.

But . . . to forget hope. Did I forget hope? Did I let it go? Or did I grope my dark way to a deeper understanding of it?

I passed through that hell gate.

And I want to say, to this newly diagnosed person, here is how hope works: you put one foot in the story of reality, and you put one foot in the land of hope. Hard hope, the kind that's full of hard truths. This is what hope looks like since my dire diagnosis: I've buried myself so many times in my mind, and yet, here I stand. I've buried many others who had no business dying. Others who dropped dead due to accident or a sudden prod of the heart. A clot thrown.

We can't know. That is what my statement of hope is, from here, on the inside of it.

We can't know.

My hope is hardened, like a scar. It's ropy. A black cord. It's raised in ridges on my skin and spelled out in the dark marks of the tattoo dots that plot the radiation field. Hope is inscribed on my body in white lines and places where my body used to be but is no more.

I have trouble, though, explaining how this hard reality works to an 11-year-old. I can't bring myself to do it. He says, "When I have kids and you're a grandma . . ."

And I say, "Yes," and then go quiet. I don't keep those conversations going.

He will have a hard scar that my sins of omissions, my disease, and my death will leave. Just like I bear the hard scars of his birthing. This is the way life is, this is reality, it's how it is.

I have no business being alive. And yet I am. This is what I would like to say. That is my statement of hope.

I have come through the dark tunnel, pill by IV pole, by dark night turned to morning, one day at a time. One foot in front of the other. Each day bound to the future and the past. Bound by the story of our love.

In fact, I'd rather speak of love than hope. Hope is a hollow place that brings me little joy. But love is abundant. I hold fast to it. It can't be torn, or rent, or mended. ✴

AMY MOORE PATERSON (1972–2018) was a writer, mother, wife, daughter, and friend. She loved cats, books, notebooks, notepads, sticky notes, index cards, basketball, tea, and reading and writing in her light-filled home in Portland, OR. Before turning to writing full-time, she had a career in marketing and cofounded the nonprofit My Little Waiting Room. She graduated with her MFA in Creative Nonfiction from Pacific University in 2018, shortly before she died of metastatic breast cancer on November 6, 2018.

Cancer is

The game changer. The life that will be forever different. The take away. The ribbons—pink, orange, purple, teal. The fucking colors. The fights, the survivors. Tough. Strong. Cancer is your teacher. It is your life lesson. It is your gateway. Your initiation. Your opportunity.

NAH. NO. Not giving it. Not doing it. It does not have that power.

Cancer is.

It is part of me. Part of life. It is one of the things that happen. It is a game changer, but I still recoil when I hear the words *survivor, fighter, we win, you will win, tough, it was your doorway.* The words come out and I recoil . . . listening, reading, ready to strike down with the venom— the poison of every cancer cell that flowed through my body, that runs through my veins like rebellious teenagers reproducing in the dark hallways of my bone marrow. The venom of a mean desperate teenager who spews at the unsuspecting niceties of fight words that the world has placed on my journey.

My journey.

You do not get to define my doorways or my gateways or my life lessons.

You do not get to put my cancer, my rebellious teenager cells, in a little box of niceties so you can make sense of your world.

This is mine. This struggle to release the teenagers—to love them, to let them find their way into maturity.

You do not know my path or the doorways I have opened. You do not know if cancer taught me a lesson or gave me lessons to learn. Cancer does not get to be a defining doorway. It is.

It is needle pokes and doctor appointments and treatments that kill me, and it is love and hummingbirds and generosity and light. Cancer gets to be life like rebellious teenagers doing what they want, saying what they feel, being who they are, and with the manumission of cultural expectations.

You need to know this about cancer.

It is my life. It is not a gateway, or a lesson—it is life and when life happens you can always choose to run, to find shade, to find a wall, to get scared, to make your world smaller, but if you listen to those rebellious adolescents—you run into the rain, your very existence challenges the system, you drive fast and you sleep late and you feel good and you cry and you yell and you swim in the river and you play hooky and you sing really loud and dance a lot and you don't notice that the world has labeled you as something. As a menace, or a renegade, and you do notice you, but a t-shirt on that says *f*ck you* to the people who want to create a platitude and give you a colored ribbon, all because they need a box of safety to make sense of their own life.

this. is. life. ✖

A Story That Needs to be Told

Damn. I don't want to write on this subject today.

Can I create a new story around death? A story that needs to be told—maybe death, in all its possibility, is waiting with vivid colors and infinite potential to speak a message of hope.

Religion offers a refuge, the promise of heaven, the story of an afterlife, the reunion of family. Maybe reality is the refuge. Maybe death is better than the present. Maybe this is death—it is evident all around us. Death brings life—the trees shed their leaves, the flowers pull back into the earth, the caterpillar sheds its coat, love morphs and grows out of pain and loss, life becomes beauty when dreams die.

He said death scared him as we discussed HIS cancer.

She said, "It's amazing what we do to stay alive."

At every turn, we are bombarded with death.

The death of a career.

The death of a loved one.

The death of a relationship.

The death of a flower.

Fear drives us to the front door of the nearest refuge.
Fear shuts the door and locks us in.

Fear teaches us the mantra of the refuge: *to live is life, to die is gain.*
What if death was the voice of freedom?
If freedom was the voice of love?
What if love drove us to face death with an open heart?
What if the open heart caused us to see each moment as the one right before death?
To see that this moment, this space—will disappear—will move—will die.

This moment—in its death—creates the next moment of life. ✢

CYNTHIA SPECKMAN was given the gift of "more" by an altruistic anonymous bone marrow donor in 2012. She now lives on the edge–literally and figuratively–residing on the North Oregon Coast. She has a strong aversion to commitment except when it comes to breaking rules, stereotypes, and the patriarchy–and then she is all in. Her claim to fame is her amazing daughter.

The Dark Forest

The fact is, I am well into the dark forest. And it looks like standing in the parking lot waiting for Craig to come off the trail, out of the woods and down from altitude. It looks like missing all the things I used to love to do, and it looks like making new memories that are sad half-steps toward what we used to love. It looks like resignation, loss, grief, less-than, and regret. It looks like tender love that finds its object fading.

The forest—the dark forest—is lonely, and that's the worst thing. It's not as frightening as it is final, disappointing, heartbreaking. Here is where things end, are shed, and what comes out the other side is leaner, stripped and dry, a last flower in early winter, dogged and not beautiful but alive still, and alone.

The dark forest is knowing that I can't walk with Craig, that I can't play in the snow, that I can't run to catch a frisbee or chase my dogs.

The dark forest is knowing I will go sooner than I want. It's facing that Craig will be alone and do you know, worse than all my self-pity and rage about what my body cannot do, is the fact that I cannot picture Craig alone. I can't allow myself to imagine him dealing with hurting because of my loss. I can't picture that grief somehow; my mind won't go to it, and so I can't imagine what this must feel like for him. I am paralyzed by the thought of it, just as I cannot begin to imagine what it would be to lose him. God, I just can't. There's no going on because there's no me without Craig.

I puzzle over what we are without each other. Of course, each of us is a whole person, but honestly the whole of me has Craig in it. There's no me without Craig. Even my childhood memories have him in them because he has seen them, heard them, has taken them in and holds them with me.

We have our own minds, our own secrets, fears, desires, our own physical pain or pleasure—we are two separate beings that belong to a single whole, identified by that whole, seen as part of it, and we feel ourselves part of that single whole, indivisible.

Which is to say: I don't know how either of us imagines going on without the other. But how I do want Craig to go on, to be the boys' father and, God willing, a grandfather.

Alive and loved and loving—that's the only way I know how to see Craig. ✔

Start Here

I am that child, fearless, alight, running into love all day.

I am that girl made by lightning. Electric, shocking.

I am my father, stiff, afraid, carrying unspoken grief, wretched before so much shame.

I am my mother, and she is her mother, fearless, fierce with loving.

I am this woman, <u>this</u> woman, this woman who keeps building a life, dreaming of life, holding onto life. ✝

KATE REDMOND is a writer in Portland, Oregon. She loves loud music and great girlfriends. She is mother to two precious sons. She has been married to her beloved Craig for nearly 35 years.

KELLY EVERETT

LOVE TO LIVE   LIVE TO LOVE

Women with breast cancer have different experiences. Having metastasized breast cancer is a game changer for your time left alive in life. I was diagnosed in 2014. Many women die within five years after a diagnosis like mine. Often when survivors share their stories, the ones who have fought more than one round of this disease over the years, you quickly observe their steel inner strength. We are fearless warriors.

My personal journey has not been without several self-reinventions, not by choice. Cancer grows in the shadows of our cells. Scans find them. Your oncologist team works to find the right treatment plan to give you more time.

What you do with your life's interruptions can be challenging. Form a cancer team with family, friends, support groups, journaling, and books to seek knowledge of your cancer. Find a new groove to fit your life. Spiritually look for guidance in nature, God, or the universe for inner peace.

Side effects—they can be tough. Daily routines are turned upside down. Brain fog. Energy depleted and more. Motivation for survival to get through another day or hour. Good news is you learn how to fight, how to save yourself, how to be resourceful, how to love yourself more, how to ask for help, and how to live with this disease.

Writing this today, I am in my third round of metastasized breast cancer that has spread to my bones again—to more areas with tumors. Last fall my chemo did not work. Scans showed no improvement. Lost time. This is part of the challenge. Chemo treatments do not always work. Cancer does not wait. Onto a new drug or treatment. Not ready to quit or take out my bucket list. Cancer has given me a razor focus on my life. It does not get easier fighting this disease. On the outside, I do not look like a woman with cancer. Except for I am breastless.

I am grateful for my husband's enduring love. I give my unconditional love to my two adult sons, who are the anchors to my soul. My beautiful sisters and BFF light my days with love, joy, private moments, and can make me laugh. Thank you to all my extended family and friends who have shared this journey with me. ✦

KELLY EVERETT lives in Portland, Oregon, with her husband, two adult sons, and two cats. She loves spending time at the ocean and in nature, camping, gardening, reading, and being with her family and watching their best lives unfold. She feels lucky to have the writing group to draw energy from and as a place to build confidence with cancer friends as she undergoes continued treatment for advanced stage breast cancer.

Cancer Etiquette

"You look too healthy to have cancer."

This is what the primary care doctor said to me as I sat there, belly extended with ascites, out of breath when I walked or talked too much. How is one supposed to look if they have undiagnosed Stage 4 ovarian cancer?

"You look great!"

This is what an acquaintance said to me after a Zoom meeting. What he can't see on my outside is my constant runny nose, my dry and unsupple skin, the swelling of my lower legs from lymphedema. Or the scar from my pubic bone, around my belly button and up to my chest, still dry and flakey in some spots, no matter how much lotion or body oil I use. And my insides, he can't know what the fight is like, cell to cell, the struggle with fatigue, that shut-down-everything kind of fatigue.

"Keep on fighting."

This is what friends say when they notice my absence after a chemo session. They don't understand what it feels like to have poison pumped into your body. The feeling like the poison is now in control as it spreads everywhere looking for cancer cells to kill and killing other good cells along the way. Collateral damage.

"I'm sure you will be fine."

This is what my oldest friend said. He's a man, so I do cut him some slack. Doesn't he know that Stage 4 ovarian cancer is not something to be fine about? That the five-year survival rate is miniscule? That no matter how strong you may think I am, this is kicking my ass! Sure, there are moments, even days, when I feel just fine. But they don't add up to anything long term.

"God never gives you more than you can handle."

Really? God gave me ovarian cancer? To prove what? That I can handle it? Not the God of MY understanding. My God says to me, cherish each moment, each encounter, look to the truth, the beauty in these encounters. Walk your own path. ❦

The Small Stuff

In the big scheme of things, isn't it all small stuff?

On a beautiful sunny day with a nice, cool ocean breeze, I found myself on a semi-secluded beach in such sorrow that tears just streamed down my face, no sobbing, just the flow of tears.

I sat on the sand, staring out to the horizon, then working my vision back to shore, watching and listening to the waves roll in. My hands in the sand, I sat upright with a handful of mostly dry, slightly damp sand. I let my fingers spread apart and watched the sand slowly flow back down to the beach, leaving only a small dab in the palm of my hand.

I looked at it, really looked at it, trying to see each individual grain of sand, really small rocks. I tried to pick just one grain of sand up. No, they were determined to stay in a bunch. Not having much in the way of fingernails that could maybe be my sand tweezers, I kept trying.

I noticed something, the tears had stopped. My whole existence was focused on the sand in the palm of my hand and my futile attempts at selecting a single grain.

As alone as I felt when I arrived at the beach, I now knew that it was me, that single grain of sand. Me amongst the rest of humanity. Nothing special when separated out by itself, but put all the grains of sand together, what a beautiful beach it made.

I was trying to find myself in the crowd, to stand out, when really the comfort of living side by side with others is to find yourself a person amongst people. ✿

Trusting Life

Yes, I am learning to trust life, as I've never done before. There are lots of stumbles, skinned knees, pebbles in my palms. I am learning to get back up, new to me as well.

Trusting life feels easier than trusting people. People disappoint, disappear. Life is always here with me.

My late husband told me he wanted me to LIVE, in all caps. I did trust him, his honesty as a dying man. I didn't understand what he meant at first.

Feeling isolated and alone after his death, during the pandemic, during chemotherapy, my mind finally saw the letters "L I V E" standing tall before me, guardians of my future, asking me to trust them, my own personal Stonehenge.

Today, life is an experience to be had, to cultivate. I see the sprouts coming up. It is unknown if they are flowers or weeds, but it doesn't matter. ✈

LOUISE SMITH is an original Oregonian, born and raised in Eugene, and currently lives in Portland with Chester, her guardian cat. She's taken writing back up in the past few years, walking the journey of pandemic, the death of her husband, and her diagnosis of Stage 4 ovarian cancer.

The Underworld of Joy

Once upon a time, long after complacency and silence were wrong, but before a time when freedom was clear, there existed The Underworld of Joy.

Unlike other Underworlds, where we go to expel demons and claim victory over Darkness, this Underworld is brilliant. It sparkles. An effervescent light. Bubbling and Tickling and Twinkling upon all who visit.

The doorway to Joy has a barrier that keeps away fear and ignorance. It only allows entry to those with Hope. Its flag flutters its welcoming tune: *Let Joy Not Escape Us*. A flag depicting Harmony, Understanding, Love, and Unity. A brain within a heart with arms embracing them, lifting them up for acceptance.

The Underworld of Joy recognizes the Reality of Balance. Recognizes that anyone having only one experience dulls one's ability to remain Curious, Experimental, Experiential. The Underworld for Joy expects those who enter to see possibility. Seek opportunity. Thrive.

Yes.

The Underworld of Joy was, is, will always be, the haven for those who feel that while so much is failing, they know better and will continue to try. ✦

Leaving

She didn't ask permission.
She didn't wait to pause.
She didn't want to risk
chickening out,
or running around like a chicken
without a head.

She didn't choose her clothing.
She didn't create the character of who she wanted to be.
She didn't open her closet doors
or decide today is a purple plush and perfect day
or green, graceful and gregarious.

No, she left her outward selves hanging on the racks
in their seasonal
order.

She didn't choose what shoes she would wear.
The wooden clogs from the mountain of Italy.
The functional comfort shoes the podiatrist prescribed.
The sneakers that make her walk worthy,
maybe even adding a little bit of jump.

She left her jewelry behind. Except for her
pearl ring, a totem to her Selfness.

She chose no scarves to flutter.
No socks to entertain her toes or
compress her aging legs.

She left behind the makeup.
The blush,
the clear foundation,
the ash reducing primer,
the double-dark black mascara,
her favorite sea blue-green smudge liner for her apple-green eyes.

The tattoos, of course,
they stayed. ✔

A Woman Going through the Experience of Cancer

Cancer is always teasing me. Either in my breasts, or an unhealed wound, or a spot on my skin that has suddenly morphed from a blotch to a fleur-de-lis.

I can be haughty about it, but that's not what's real. Haughty is naughty, an attempt to override my fear with aggressive arrogance. A full throttle, *LOOK AT ME!!!* (then the ghostly whisper of *you may never get another chance*).

After each second, and sometimes third, mammogram, each MRI, subsequent ultrasound; after each piercing of my skin for another needle biopsy, the waiting is a long dive into darkness where I desperately project illumination and faith onto the path I walk from the doctor's office to the mailbox, or the phone call when the findings are finally disclosed.

The one time I heard, "You've got cancer," the world altered so rapidly my foothold slipped. The darkness had a trap door which slid from beneath my feet, and I plummeted into the depths of *death possibly, dealing differently definitely.*

Yet no matter how long and deep the plunge into the cold harshness of my own mortality, I couldn't remain huddled in a ball at the bottom, waiting to die.

The stunningness of it, the sharp bright blades of scare struck me, stung me, stimulated my *get-up-off-your-ass-and-do-something* rage.

Calls followed—my eyes on Google, websites, "what does LCIS mean?"

Finally, summoning up my courage, I called Alan, an old friend who is a breast cancer researcher. I trusted him to present even the worst

worst-case scenario so it would penetrate my terror with the tenderness and simplicity of 25 years of friendship.

"It's like a freckle. Autopsies have shown that almost everyone has LCIS. It's when it changes that you have to worry. Yes, with your history you need to be careful, comprehensive in your awareness. The good news is, right now you are cancer free."

I had choices to make—not about surgery, but about preventative care. My father's family's propensity for all sorts of cancer, though primarily breast cancer in men and women, puts me at high risk. I tested free of BRACA genes. All the new changes in my breasts were scar tissue, calcifications, cysts. This year's series—first abnormal—was eventually determined to be a new and unusual cluster of cysts beneath the nipple of my left breast. To be watched for sure, but not with the wary eye of a hawk.

So, I breathe a bit more easily, dutifully doing weekly self-breast exams, and visits for a second opinion when a lump feels different.

Yet always in the back of my head, the gnawing never leaves. *What will I do if cancer comes and stays?* Do I know the answer? Will I dance through the fear, into acknowledgment, and then take action? It's what I've always done. I'm certainly planning to. ❦

MARGIE ANN STANKO is a woman. A writer. A former dancer. A graduate of One Spirit Interfaith Seminary (2013), she is an ordained interfaith minister and certified spiritual counselor. She operates Tea & Stones: Creative Meditative Experiences. Margie celebrates all of life's transitions and offers spiritual companioning. She has been a member of the OHSU Writing Group for Women Healing from Cancer since 2020.

Anxiety

"Living with anxiety is like being followed by a voice. It knows all your insecurities and uses them against you. It gets to the point when it's the loudest voice in the room. The only one you can hear." ✯

~ AUTHOR UNKNOWN

Tyler chose this piece to share because these words resonate with his experience and inspire his inner writer.

Buried

My words won't come out.

They get stuck in my mind.

And when they play hard to get

they get harder to find.

I want to speak up

but my words hold on tight

to a standard that says

they must come out "just right."

So they stay hidden deep

in my mind and I know:

if I can't learn to share

then I can't learn to grow.

~ BY JESSY HUMANN

Tyler chose this piece to share because these words resonate with his experience and inspire his inner writer. "Buried" is reprinted here with the kind consent of the poet (http://www.heartpocketpoems.com/blog/buried).

TYLER ROULETTE likes to re-enact his favorite movies and TV shows. He also likes to watch and play video games, listen to music, and go for walks whenever the weather is nice. Tyler has a passion for animals and archery.

New Begin

A darkness like night as it shuttles my life

Years passing by as the stars all cry

For the women who are filled with despair

She remembers them for they are part of me

I often wonder if they remember me

We once had a joy we craved to share

We all had achievements that were based on theirs

At the end we will all be there once again

Broken Glass

My life is shattered like broken glass

How can I convince myself that it all still matters?

I kneel on my knees and try to mend

Like a puzzle searching for the piece to begin

Looking and searching who will be my friends

Like a running river that never ends

✦

ROBIN WELSH has three beautiful daughters. She is a great grandmother of three and has nine grandchildren. Robin is a cancer survivor and has written a book while going through cancer treatments. She relocated back to Tigard, Oregon, four years ago. She has been a volunteer minister now for 30 years. Most of Robin's employment has circled around working with young children. She is currently a program counselor. Robin loves book writing, playing guitar, harmonica, African Drumming, meditation, yoga, a tai chi dance form, and animals.

Elegy
for My Younger Sister

I.
Knowing

Not knowing
She checked her wristwatch

Beethoven's notes spilling out
She played the Pathétique
On the mourning black upright piano
Her fingers hesitated
On those white and black keys!

Knowing
The purity of death
Secrets of the Women's Script*

She again checked her wristwatch

Is death like falling
Falling asleep
Next to a child playing while
Humming a happy simple tune?

II.

I am a heap of bones.

The entire pile of me assumes
The saltiness of Job's tear—
The grain growing unattended
On the beach near a fishing village.

The cremator wears a pair of gray gloves.

In his movement, he seems he has an eternity
He picks me up and
Places me piece
By piece
Into the urn.

He is good at what he is doing.

The last piece he puts into the urn is my skull,
An intact piece of me—
The parietal bone, occipital attached. ❧

*Women's Script is a variation of Chinese characters that was used exclusively
among women in Hunan province, Jiangyong County of southern China.

STELLA JENG GUILLORY lives in Vancouver, Washington. Her poetry has appeared in *Bamboo Ridge, The Hawaii Writers' Quarterly, La'ila'i, Sister Stew: Fiction and Poetry by Women, VoiceCatcher* (Winter 2013 and Summer 2015), *Just Now: 20 New Portland Poets, America the National Catholic Review* (2014 and 2015), *Verseweavers, PoetryMoves,* and *RE: VISION POEMS.* Her poem, "Chief Joseph's Flute," was awarded second place by the *Hawaii Review* for the Ian MacMillan Writing Award for Poetry in 2016. Her chapbook, *An Advancing Glacier,* was published by Moonstone Press, based in Philadelphia, in 2019.

Changed

Something changed.

Nothing mattered.

Everything shifted.

Something showed up in my life taking the form of cancer. It brought with it a group of friends, including fear, anxiety, depression, anger, and regret. It roared into my life and took up residence like a pack of wild animals, with no respect for what it trampled and devoured. Something took parts of my physical body. Something tried to take parts of my mind, and it did for far too long. Something changed my life.

Nothing that used to be normal felt important. It seemed as if the world was full of irrelevant and mindless activities. Life reminded me of a merry-go-round. There was a lot of motion swirling by me but I never went anywhere. Things that were part of my usual routine no longer seemed like how I should spend my time. It was easier to say no to expectations placed upon me, even those I put there myself. Nothing changed my life.

Everything was different. My priorities were made clear. I saw my time as more valuable, and I became intentional about how I spent it. I worked on end-of-life paperwork and plans. I spent a lot of time reflecting and wondering if I'd done my best with my life. I developed a new perspective and realized I was done with surviving life, and I was ready to thrive. I had neglected myself for far too long, and it was time to wake up and live. Everything changed my life.

I am different, but better. I will never be the same person I was. I don't want to be. ✦

I Was Robbed

For two weeks, I was a cancer patient, without cancer, and nobody knew. It was my secret.

Sally, Charlie Brown's little sister, is famous for screeching, "I've been robbed!" when she missed out on Halloween by waiting with Linus for The Great Pumpkin. I relate to her, but I wasn't missing the fun stuff. I never *got* to say, "I have cancer." Before surgery, I told people, "I'm having abdominal surgery for a precancerous stage of endometrial cancer."

By the time I received the diagnosis, the tumor was out of my body. "I have cancer," never escaped my lips. Instead, I was left with, "I had cancer." People focused on *had* while I focused on *cancer*. I will be a cancer patient for three years. I am a cancer survivor. That sounds foreign.

I never went through the stages of grief. I now describe it as having had something evil and deadly inside me. I am left with the past-tense version. I HAD cancer. While I had been dismissive, a few people reminded me I could have died if this was left undiagnosed.

People celebrated my successful surgery and moved on. The celebration period was over before I got the hard news.

This left me with nobody to call on, nobody to talk through it with, and nobody to come sit with me, put their arms around me, or cry with me. I'm not faulting anyone; I would have had the same response. We celebrated the good . . . and it was good. "They got it all," were wonderful words, but I still felt the unspoken weight.

I felt guilty for not being grateful, and simply moving forward. I was angry as I tried to accept the news and process it. I was sad and felt alone. I still have the fears common for cancer patients, but I experience guilt by comparing my story to the battle stories of others. I want to scream from a mountaintop, "I had *expletive* cancer!" I want the world to stop for a minute and acknowledge me. Then we can all move on together. ✦

People matter to **LOIS FLORES**, and she loves to encourage those she meets. You can often find her by listening for her laugh. Lois has a daily battle between her left and right brain, as they fight like siblings for equal time.

A Forethought of Grief

From Wendell Berry's poem about wild things, this short phrase stands out: *"forethought of grief."* I think that's very much where I was stuck this winter and early spring, thinking about grief much more than I care to.

Recently, my oncologist and I discussed the possibility that I might be experiencing some PTSD at this point, after ten months or so of ongoing treatment since my diagnosis of Multiple Myeloma last June. The physical impact of the stem cell transplant in December of last year was particularly traumatic, though not the actual transplant itself, which is somewhat anticlimactic, but rather the overwhelming effects of the chemo given just before that procedure. I was very nauseated, weak, and tired during the two and a half weeks I spent in the hospital, and those symptoms continued at home for nearly a full month, with much time and effort invested in regaining my strength and appetite.

I wonder now if what I've experienced is, in fact, much bigger than just coping with the recent trauma, which is tough enough, to include a stronger sense of my mortality. That's a bone-chilling realization. I know a cancer diagnosis can make one reevaluate one's life and reorder priorities, which is a good thing, but it has made me very aware that I won't live forever. Now I find myself wondering just how long I have on this earth. There is still so much I want to do! I haven't lost many of my interests. While I'm feeling much better physically at this point, and my oncologist is pleased with my progress, my mind and spirit have lagged behind, needing more time to process all that's happened and what it might mean for my future. ✤

One World

Keeping in mind the idea of one world can be particularly challenging for me, but also a healthy and helpful reminder for someone who's experienced a strong sense of isolation and loneliness at times during this cancer journey. I've often felt frightened and alone just contemplating the fact that friends and relatives may not get what it's been like for me to be poked and prodded, tested frequently, and infused with powerful chemicals, unable to travel far from home for more than a day or two in the past year because of frequent oncology appointments and being immunocompromised.

Now that I'm past the initial stage of treatment for Multiple Myeloma and ready to embark on maintenance, with fingers crossed for a full remission, I'm able to take more interest in friends' and relatives' lives and keep up with what's happening around the world. Doing so reminds me how lucky I am in many respects and that there are many, many people living in dire circumstances. They may not have cancer, but they are nevertheless experiencing life-threatening conditions. The plight of the Ukrainian people readily comes to mind as I write this, but they're certainly not the only ones living in constant fear.

It's important to me that I remain aware that I don't have a monopoly on suffering. That frees me up to start living more fully in the world again, among others and do what little I can to help, whether it's making a donation or volunteering my time and energy. I'm happiest when I am able to direct my gaze outward into this one world we share. ✝

FRANCIE MEYERS is a retired educator and current Airbnb host living in SW Portland with her husband, Peter, and dog, Gracie. Their daughter, Ellen, is grown and lives out of state, working as a journalist. Francie loves to read and has wide-ranging interests in literature, but also likes to make time to write, in addition to pursuing other hobbies such as gardening, traveling, attending plays and concerts, and trying out new recipes.

hang on in
this moment
for the ride

I remember/don't remember

I remember getting the call from the doctor, waiting for the news, hoping for the answer, dreading the answer.

I don't remember what I was wearing that Monday morning when I heard the doctor's voice—not the nurse's, the doctor's—and I knew.

I remember waiting for surgery. The wait, longer than expected. My dad's nervousness filled the room, covering my own, covering me with protection. Finally, being moved to the operating room, the anesthesiologist joking how many beers did I want his drugs to equal.

I don't remember the recovery room, when I woke up, how I woke up, arriving in the hospital room, the name of my nurse who told me that my pee would be blue because of the dyes, a comedic pause in the seriousness of it all.

I remember my first words after surgery were about how many drains I had, the answer telling me if the cancer had spread. The kids coming to visit with my parents, looking so small, scared, and excited they got to eat hot dogs in the cafeteria.

I don't remember the drive home, arriving home, landing in the chair that was to be just mine for the next week or so. In only 28 hours everything had changed, and nothing had changed.

I remember my six-year-old asking me when my breast would grow back.
I don't remember if I laughed or cried.

I remember not remembering. I remember remembering. Are they the
same? Are they different? The circle of the memories continuously
moving, some lost, some added, while others remain. ◄

Something to hold on to/let go of

We have learned that saying good-bye is not an end.

We have learned that letting go does not make you fall.

We have learned holding on too tight can cause a crack.

We have learned that not knowing brings more possibilities.

We have learned that knowing is always temporary.

We have learned that light, no matter how small, will win over darkness.

We have learned when one is afraid, one can still take a step
letting the fear walk beside us, not in front.

We have learned that missing someone always hurts, and also
will often bring a smile, if we wait long enough.

We have learned that healing can happen at any step of the journey.

We have learned letting go is not forgetting, nor giving up, but
a reaching in and a reaching out—completing the circle—
no beginning, no end. ⨕

Hair

I'm going to lose my hair, I cried to my kids.

They knew it was a possibility, but now it was really happening.

Chunks of it had just fallen out in the shower.

My hair is falling out, I sobbed.

My son was quiet, looking on, stating, *It's okay. It's going to be okay*—
his mantra throughout it all.

My daughter shrieked, *That is so weird!*

Then she paused, an impish look forming—*Can I touch your head
when you're bald?* ✦

S is a daughter, sister, wife, mother, friend, psychotherapist, traveler,
books and languages, grateful and curious, and a breast cancer

It's not fair, Snoopy. It's just not fair.

More than forty years later, I can't hear the word "fair" without thinking of Snoopy and the night we snuggled up bemoaning the unfairness of being sent to bed early for no good reason. It was the premiere of *Little House on the Prairie*. The show ran an hour, a full thirty minutes past my bedtime. Though I could have watched the first half, my parents sent me to bed early. As I lay in bed with Snoopy, I could hear the TV below me as the rest of the family watched. Lucy came through my room, heard my crying and the immortal line—"It's not fair Snoopy, it's just not fair."

It still isn't. But it is what it is. Why do I have this cancer? I've led a pretty good life. It's not fair. Is it something that I have instead of another? Well, maybe that makes it more fair. But maybe not. Snoopy may know, but he's not talking. ✦

Snoopy, a childhood best friend, went to the afterlife with Betsy on January 28, 2019.

7/18/17

Two years ago, I might have said hummingbirds were cool, but I didn't really think about them much. This all changed last summer because of cancer—mine and my sister's.

Two weeks after my surgery and diagnosis, my sister was diagnosed with breast cancer. One day, lying in bed, she heard the crows outside her window and recalled the Northwest Coast Indian tales of the trickster Raven, plucking the sun out of the box and releasing it into the world. She thought the imagery was perfect for her—and imagined Raven plucking her little tumor out of her breast.

I decided to get her earrings and searched the web for the perfect Northwest Coast artist's rendition of Raven. I also bought myself a pair of earrings while I was there—mine depicted hummingbirds. Those earrings started my obsession with these remarkable creatures.

The earrings came with an explanation of Hummingbird's role in ancient folklore. He is a messenger. A carrier of well wishes. "In times of sorrow and pain, he is known for bringing joy and healing."

My mom and sisters bought me hummingbird attractant flowers and plants for my deck and a feeder I could hang on the window. I saw my first visitor to the feeder shortly after receiving a hateful text from an estranged longtime friend who had apparently heard of my diagnosis and sent a message—"Just. Joyful. I"—to me, years after our last communication. As I sat there crying, I looked up and saw the hummingbird telling me that I was surrounded by joy and love and healing and well-wishers.

The obsession grew from there—kitchen and bathroom towels, Northwest Coast prints, another Oaxacan hummingbird, puzzles, books, more earrings, stickers, temporary tattoos, car decals, a carved Northwest Coast wall hanging, Christmas ornaments, and the list goes on. Many came with their own explanations of the positive energy and support brought by hummingbirds.

I now have three hummingbird feeders and several visitors that come to my patio regularly.

All these hummingbirds—real and depicted in art and practical items—bring the wonder of the world and joy and healing to me. ✦

ELIZABETH SHIPPEN AMES (1968–2019)—known to all as Betsy—was born in Bangkok, Thailand, the youngest of four kids. Her joy in travel, love for family (and friends who felt like family), endless curiosity, and commitment to her community marked her fifty years. We were lucky to have her in our lives, and fortunate that she lives on in her writings, her photography, and our memories.

4/13/2016

On May 14th, 2013 I was wearing a bright red knit beanie with a little green stem on top. It was meant to look like an apple.

It was given to me in September of the previous year. A gift Matt had drawn out for months, maybe years. He said it was perfect for me. He beamed from ear to ear. I may be remembering this wrong—me conflating this occasion with another. He's given me more than one knit hat. He's pleased with himself in either example. It's "perfect for me" in either example, but in the occasion with the apple hat, I don't entirely understand why. I don't even own any other knit hats except the ones he gave me. And I don't often eat apples.

The hats came in handy when I lost my hair. By the end, they were covering a creepy, molting-bird look I'd been rocking for too long while hair kept falling out. I had dyed my hair a maroon color. Sometimes I find those hairs on the insides of hats, still, as I no longer wear them with any frequency.

Anyway, back to May 14th. I was a maroon-colored molting bird in a knit hat shaped like an apple. I was at my friend Ryan's house, and he looked at me and said, "You know . . . I've never seen you without a hat on."

That was true. So, so, intentionally true. We'd met while I was sick, and though I was now "technically better," my body somehow looked more sickly than ever.

He wanted to see it. I warned him about the whole situation—I don't remember his response or how I felt about it, only that I removed my hat. He assessed the look of it briefly, and then said, "Okay we're doing something about this."

I was marched straight into his bathroom. He got out his electric razor and in very little time at all I was a brand-new, shiny, powerful bald.

The next day I drove to Seattle and had lunch with Matt. He grinned from ear to ear and stroked my scalp. It appealed to his punk rock sensibilities to be out with a bald girl. "It's perfect for you," he said. ✦

1/9/2019

Drowning is a lot like flying.
You're weightless, floating, drifting, surrounded by blue. You're out of your element.
Nobody will see you if they're not looking.

Finally, your spine isn't doing the work of holding the weight of your body.

Your feet are no longer burdened with standing.

Your hair whips around you, uncivilized, unruly, impossible to tame.

You're not going anywhere, just everywhere at once. You're getting lost in something larger than yourself now. Something that connects everybody. Something that feels infinite, but isn't.

Something integral to living can kill you. You can have too much of something you need. Surrounded in blue and aimless, adrift, somebody said it was a superpower. Somebody told you it made you strong. But it's blue around you, your feet find no solid ground, and you don't feel powerful. Just cold. ✦

7/3/2017

There are two of me, and one of them is channel surfing.

"And why?!" the other me asks. "We have the internet now; you can watch anything you want any time."

Other me scoffs, "That's why channel surfing is so special—it's so rare that we're even around cable anymore."

"We're on vacation."

"300 channels of senseless trash. Unsolved crimes, infomercials, music videos! This _is_ vacation."

One me looks at the other with head-shaking, arms-crossed, disappointed mother eyes. "You can't just sit there all day."

The other me, knowing the card up her sleeve, remains undaunted. "I've done it before. Never underestimate my ability to idle."

The first me—arguably the more sensible me, lets out a fly-swatty groan. "Please, you are _not_ talking about the cancer again."

Again, second me fires back her signature scoff. "I'll talk about it if I want to."

"Well," says first me, "I'm sure that space age juicer for $29.99 will be a big help to you on that."

"Do you think so?"

"No."

"They include five extra cups and a bag to put them in if I call now."

"Change the channel."

"I'm glad we agree on channel surfing,"

In the momentary black reflection of the TV screen, one me looks at the other. She doesn't sigh outwardly but hears her own indignation rumble from inside out. It's sunny out. Beautiful, even. September.

"Don't be so dramatic," she says to herself, and her self wavers.

"I didn't mean because of the cancer," she says half-joking. "It's just that it's almost fall."

Sunlight is a stream through the window. It is never almost fall. I ignore myself in the mirror as I put on a hat and go outside. ✦

BRIANNA BARRETT is a playwright, screenwriter, and performance artist from Portland, Oregon. She led the OHSU Writing Group for Young Adults Healing from Cancer from 2016 to 2019. Her theatrical work has been developed at Artists Repertory Theatre, the Eugene O'Neill National Playwriting Conference, Theatre 33, HART Theatre, and the Fertile Ground Festival. Her short plays are published by Samuel French/Concord Theatricals and Applause Books. Called "Portland's Best Storyteller" by *Willamette Week*, she has performed at festivals like Pickathon and her own limited series podcast with Bag & Baggage Productions. She has an MFA in playwriting from UCLA.

DEBORAH BROD

My Mom as Botticelli's Venus

So, I just heard my mother will *not* be leaving with my brother tomorrow to stay a few weeks in Florida with him. He just told me he was at the end of his rope in dealing with her. I've been at that point for a few years now, my life going out with the tides of her life, and *not* coming back in, refreshed. Going out, not coming back in. You can imagine—no matter how much I love my mother and how close we've been, including sharing a rare chronic blood cancer they used to say was even rarer, hereditarily speaking—that after almost six years as her voluntary full-time/part-time caregiver, I was looking forward to a little break, a chance to *not* feel the tug of that umbilical connection for a few weeks, and to know that she's safe, and maybe even having fun in that famous, infamous Florida sun! And to see, just see: what would emerge now from my chrysalis—too fine a word!—my caterpillar of a life?

But instead, I see an image of Botticelli's Venus—emerging magically from that improbably regal shell on that warm, placid ocean's shore—surrounded by her breathy admirers, fanning the flames of her pale, mystical, otherworldly beauty. My mother has been obsessed with this version of Venus for as long as I can remember (collecting replicas and permutations, in all media and sizes, from Italian postcards of the painting to a quarter-life-sized plaster sculpture that she faces whenever she sits down to eat). She revealed recently that many years ago, newly married, someone once told her that *she*—my mother-to-be!—reminded him of *her, this Venus*! Aha! And so, surreptitiously soaked in, marinated . . . and eventually, voilà, Botticelli's Venus (the central figure of his painting "The Birth of Venus," c. 1485, 450 years before my mother was born) became her aspirational avatar!

So now, to temporarily escape, or assuage, this family crisis, I see her, my mother/Botticelli's Venus, young and virginal, on the shore of this placid, beyond-calm ocean—maybe not in Florida—relaxed but poised, standing up so straight (her chronic back problems obliterated, washed away), with a backdrop of those waters, eternally tranquil, and like her early spring birthstone, limpid aquamarine . . . unperturbed and imperturbable, unrufflable . . . impossibly serene! ✦

Snake Lesson

I cannot describe the slow, slow way it moved, that snake I saw at noon today, twisting, and hugging the bamboo. But it seems in a way similar to my tortuous efforts at processing the past few years with my mother—her chronic blood cancer, her spine issues, her erratic emotions, her unpredictable lashing-out—and myself, same cancer, same spine issues, my own variable, volatile feelings. I wish I could race through it all cleanly, swiftly, the wind with me, like a fox or a rabbit, or fly above it like a bird, or a dragonfly, or even a fly. But here I am, fascinated and repelled by that snake. Yes, it was graceful, and it had me transfixed. But similarly, I feel captivated, maybe captured, by my own difficulty—feels like immobility—as I painstakingly plod my way through my prickly past and present.

Let me slither out of my own skin, relishing the slithering, and into the future. ✦

Sigh Manifesto (in three haiku)

Allow those sighs to

multiply, gathering gale force,

churning stale waters,

Overturning your

doubts, years of fears, flinging up

stuff, encrusted pearls,

Which this time, you must

trust, as a sign you've landed,

you accept your depths. ✦

DEBORAH BROD is the mother of a daughter, Naomi, and the daughter of a mother, Ruth, from whom she inherited a rare chronic blood cancer, polycythemia vera. Deb is a visual artist, and her concern for our earth underlies all her work in various media, including installations made from re-purposed textiles. She teaches art to people of all ages, from toddlers to octogenarians. She also likes words sometimes! She is grateful to have serendipitously joined the OHSU Writing Group for Women Healing from Cancer in early 2021. She believes the arts are therapy we can't live without.

Pondering the Body Electric

Click on the test results,

watch the numbers:

white blood count low,

red blood count low,

neutrophils low,

protein low. All signs

of life—my life—

in this moment, going

through chemo. Again.

The story it tells about

the strength of my body, living

with this, surviving.

I see the subtle changes—

more precisely—I feel them

in my body. My words

to my daughter last night:

How can I feel so much joy

while being aware that I'm dying? ❧

In the Hospital in the Time of Covid

This day, I sit on the hospital bed. No one visits
in the time of COVID. No hands touch mine.
No smiles visible. No one breathes life with me.

My legs swell. After my shower,
after I crawl carefully back into bed,
after I cover myself with blankets,
I hit the call button.
When the nurse arrives, I ask:
Can someone put on my compression socks?
She replies she'll send in the CNA. Then is out the door.

Unknown minutes pass. Dozing
when the CNA arrives, she uncovers my legs,
grabs powder, pats it on my right foot.
Her powdery hand caresses my calf,
tears trickle from my eyes.

She takes the sock, gathers it,
rolls it between her hands.
Then carefully draws it over toes,
stretches it over the heel, lets the sock out,
tugs it over the calf, smooths it up to the knee.
Thank you for your kindness.
She goes around the end of the bed
and begins anew on my left leg.
Tears continue to flow.
When she finishes, I tell her:
There's such power in human touch.
She turns smiling eyes to me as she leaves.

Unpredictable

Anxiety and panic slither their way into the air,
wriggle into conversations:

Talk of it wriggles into nearly every conversation:

- *No. We have no hand sanitizer.*

- *Masks won't help, will they?*

- *I should've traded one of those bottles of soap for hand lotion.*

- *You're not still going to the Galapagos, are you?*

- *Don't touch that ball, Timmy!*

- *What do you mean, there's no toilet paper?!?*

It permeates the air like smoke. Its own kind of viral infection.

At the core of it, the unknown. That insecure uncertainty ~
stock market toppling, bonds wandering off target, large gatherings
(SxSW, tech shows, March Madness, Portland Symphony) canceled,
museums and libraries and schools, all closed. Omens of panic . . .
tumbling everyone. A cycle increasingly unrecognizable.

How does all that relate to cancer, to *my* cancer. The unknowns
of what my body created, how it responded to treatment,
what it may ~ or may not ~ be doing now.

I want to roar at people, *We all want predictable!* We all want to know
one day follows the next with regularity, with certainty.
When life crumples ~ and it will every now and again ~ we have choice.
Mine? To hang on, in this moment, for the ride.

HESYKHIA, a pen name for Mary-Lynne Monroe, lives with her husband, daughter, and two cats in Wilsonville, Oregon. She writes poetry, memoir, flash fiction, and nonfiction. She's published in *Offerings: Poems Written During Tiferet Journal's Spiritual Poetry Class, Vol. 2 & 3*, and the upcoming *Vol. 4; 2020 Writing from Inlandia;* and *Opening the Gate, an anthology.*

Writings from 2021

Three Chickadees ~ April 6

The chickadees living in the ugly bush, which I really should trim, are often flitting about as I watch TV. Their eager flights knock the branches against the window. They make me happy every time I notice them. Mom always called my sisters and I here "three little chickadees." I feel like those little birds are reminding me to get off the couch and do something happy, or at least productive. Despite thousands of miles, my family is always here supporting and inspiring me to be the "real" me, not the depressed me.

May 4

My grandparents had one of those Jesus prints of the footprints in the sand in their bathroom. The parable of Him being beside you and then carrying you. I often read and reread it. Many times in my life, I felt like no one was really walking beside me on my life's journey. Well, family didn't count in my mind. No one that "chose" me.

Then for years in college and beyond, I was surrounded by many diverse, interesting, compelling footprints. It took many years and many hardships for me to see that many of those footprints were shallow. Or they wandered off from me.

Now I look around me. I picture my footprints in the snow, not the traditional sand. (I love seeing my cat's footprints, knowing where he goes in winter.)

Now I see the footprints that are deep, that never strayed away, never missed a step alongside of me. My family, my husband, a few dear friends. I hope I never look at clear, crisp, icy snow beside my tracks. I want to hear the crunch of their boots trudging beside me.

Excerpted from May 11

Destroy is the goal. Yet to destroy cancer can sometimes destroy parts of you. Not only the pieces physically cut out. Some pieces of soul, of strength. Physical strength for sure. Some mental strength. Some emotional strength. It's a difficult balance. It's unnatural to assume we can only destroy what we want. ❦

Writings from 2022

Signs of Spring ~ March 15

When I open the front door to let the cats in or out, I see the snowbells blooming. They have wandered far, it seems, from wherever their original home might have been. When I'm taken outside to be loaded up for another trip to see the doctor, I can see some still in the old flower beds. Not many. Not a particular grouping to represent their origin. Those sweet snowbells seem a little less exciting. Less special somehow. Perhaps it's the depressing background of the unkept flowerbeds. Perhaps it is their predictability. Of course, they should live between the stone pavers and the front of the house. For whatever reason, I prefer the snowbells which have popped up randomly amongst the lush, bright green of our uncut grass. They seem so free and unpredictable. Perhaps I see them differently simply because I can see them from the doorway. All on my own.

Instructions On Not Giving Up ~ April 5

After Ada Limón

I wish I could find clear, concise, intelligent, well-rounded, easy-to-follow instructions written with a balance of light-hearted fun, and sincere gravity on how "Not to Give Up."

It would have to be very adaptable, as most days present a multitude of interwoven possibilities. Endless choices would have to be presented, each individual choice carrying the possibility of holding me up and hurtling me forward strongly and confidently, despite any perceived limitations, impracticalities, discouragements, or frustrations. Each choice would also have to carry the possibility of failure, of trying to prove that there is no point in trying, declaring the inevitable is there, and everyone else sees it.

If such a set of instructions did exist, I would NOT give up until I obtained a hard cover, spiral bound, signed, first edition.

Friday, May 27th

—Excerpted from a text Kelly sent family and friends two days before she died

I have very big news. It's good news this time.

I walked 25 feet. WithOUT any aid!!!

Yes, I "free walked," as I've been calling it!

My PT was holding my back brace and spotting me, I did really well. No wobbles or anything, I just went very slowly.

It was impromptu. I was doing exercises at the kitchen sink and sidesteps, reaching for stuff holding onto the counter, which we just started last week.

Then he had me let go of the counter . . .

Anyway, I went through the dining room to the living room! I touched the doorway into the dining room and went so carefully over the threshold. It suddenly seemed huge, even though it's not.

When I sat down in my chair, I just burst into tears! So shocked. So proud. So elated . . .

I still have a lot more work to do and strength and balance to build up. But this is certainly huge . . .

And I didn't get here alone. Thank you for all of the support and encouragement this year as I deal with all of the things that come up with this crazy cancer situation! I am very grateful for the love and positivity I've gotten from so many people! I can't express how much it means to me. Thank you. ✝

KELLY ANN WALSH (1977–2022) was a lover of life's adventures. Nothing was better to her than a bustling kitchen with pots and pans, all busy on the stove, or preparing a meal that brought loved ones together. Her best days were filled with cooking, kitchen-dancing, camping, hiking, writing, reminiscing, gardening, a good conversation, time with her loving husband, dear friends and family. Kelly loved seeing people loving life (and loved it even more if she could join in)! Kelly fought breast cancer beginning in the Fall of 2019, enduring chemo, multiple surgeries, radiation, and a recurrence that left her in a wheelchair for the last few months of her life. Through it all she found joy, endurance, perseverance, strength from above, and true peace.

Cancer is a Titan

—March 14, 2014

Cancer is a Titan. He owns a large fraction of humanity's health, but always seeks more. His motto is: *Our business is growth and more is never quite enough.*

Cancer dresses for his part in a variety of costumes and guises, often looking very sinister and greedy, like Snidely Whiplash on steroids. I'm walking down the street of life, minding my own business, walking a healthy walk, avoiding trap doors and other risk factors. I've heard of this guy Cancer but never expected to meet him on my street.

"I've decided to develop some real estate in your chest; we will be building several condos and a strip mall," Cancer says.

I say, "This real estate is not for sale, at any price, and the right of ownership is enforced by the Rule of Law, according to the Constitution of this Body. I will fight this development of yours to my very last breath." ❈

Originally published in "Rest in the Eye of the Storm" by Martin David Crouch (2020).

Competition

—August 25, 2017

We visited the Riverview Cemetery one morning, Doyle and I.

I dragged Doyle there with me—truth be told. I'm the owner of a green burial plot, and I wanted to see my plot and its surroundings in the morning sun from the east.

Although the hour was early, a couple of parties were already at the site, evidently an early graveside service and a couple visiting a recently interred love one with their dog.

I was also looking for a sign of completion—meaning a sign that Eddy and I had completed the arrangements for a final rest in a good way.

I looked up the hillside and remarked to Doyle: "Ah look a coyote!" It was loping through the midst of the people and their pets with such obvious self-confidence. You can always recognize a coyote—even if you don't think you have ever seen one before. They are never frightened, just there, immune to danger and above the fray.

Yes, I recognized my sign, the age-old sign of the trickster, the shape-shifting presence of the coyote. May he safely inhabit this place forever. ⨏

Originally published in "Rest in the Eye of the Storm" by Martin David Crouch (2020).

MARTY CROUCH (1947–2017) was an electrical engineer, a manager, a life coach, an entrepreneur, a husband, a father, a friend, and a lifelong learner. He lived with metastatic melanoma for the last four years of his life. Marty utilized the Oregon Death with Dignity Act and after self-administering the prescribed lethal medication surrounded by friends and family, he died in his home on September 11, 2017 at age 70.

RUTH SELID

A Just-Fun Life Experience

In my twenties, I had a dream of sailing a large, strong boat across the ocean, off for an indefinite adventure in lush lands. Then it occurred to me that perhaps I should first learn how to sail.

I signed up for a beginner's class through Portland Parks, from a downtown dock. Running down after work one night a week, we changed clothes and took out across the Willamette River until darkness caught us. The dinghies were twelve feet long and had two sails. We took turns in pairs learning how it all worked. Did I mention that I am terrified of being flung into bodies of water, however narrow or shallow, and these boats were quite tipsy? Motivation supplied, I gradually and carefully found out how to keep the boat going and in the right direction whether at helm or as crew. Oh, the joy when I could 'read' the wind and the river and let the sail go while pushing the tiller over, smoothly coming about onto a new tack.

On our graduation night, those who wanted could sail down the river to a floating restaurant for a fish-and-chips supper, and then back until, in darkness, we would get pulled the rest of the way by our teacher in a motorboat. There were enough boats, so she offered to let us go solo. My hand shot up! I was excited to be on my own and over a longer distance, handling the tiller and lines and choosing the course. I felt at one with the boat, the river, the air. At the dock, I smartly came to and tied up, and stood on the dock, mistress of my own craft.

How Relationships with Family have Changed Over Time with my Cancer

My three sisters each have played significant roles in my life as we grew up and now with my cancer diagnosis. My older sister was the one I looked up to, beautiful and smart, musically talented. I followed her to university and listened to her advice. Then our lives began to diverge as I found my own way and made a different path. My second sister was the one to be jealous of, her easy popularity and prettiness. I tried to boss her around because I was two years older. But she was lively and mischievous and had her own way of growing up. The third sister, being five years younger, was only an occasional distraction who I might be asked to help. She seemed pleasant enough but hardly a personality at thirteen when I was eighteen and ready to spread my wings.

Now in my travels with cancer and as mature adults, our roles have shifted, rather like a puzzle where one part moves aside, another comes to the fore, and another part rises to fill a space.

The older role model has become an opposite to me, our values and beliefs nearly contrary, especially with her refusal to be vaccinated against COVID-19. We communicate at a distance, and now I worry about her health. The second sister has become a close friend, sharing occasional "sister-days," she and her husband committed to spending weekends with me after coming to the end of a treatment cycle. They helped with my move to a more accessible home.

The Little Sister has emerged as a true friend and valued adviser with her experience in nursing and her no-nonsense attitude. She has come to stay for several days after the end of each treatment cycle, when I am most weak and needing rest and care. Our beliefs are not perfectly aligned, but we share core values and a sense of fun. She nudges me to nap again while she sweeps my floors. She is the one who can look the dragon square in the eye and make the effective parry, with her other arm around me. ✦

Talking to the Dead

Some days I hear my mom, a soft sound in my waiting ear, almost a voice. Some days while doing the dishes or other ordinary movements, I have an urge to call out to her, "Mom, you know what I was thinking . . ."

Other days I want to phone, ask her about that thing I am sure she knows, how to do something, what that was she told me the other day. I want to tell her something to make her smile. Across the room now, I see her. She is in three photos so characteristic, such smiles: she and I together, she and Dad, and she and Mark.

In that last one, Mark and Mom and also Rachel and I were on a ferry to see the small town on a far north Norwegian fjord where her father was born. She and I had each visited, separately, and found the old white church locked. This time it was open, and a warden was on hand to confirm the age and presence of the family in church records, so she knew it was where he had been baptized.

There is a picture of her by the baptismal font, a transcendent smile. Photos nudge the memories to the front of my attention, but it is the background voice I treasure, the unbidden sense that she is just out of sight. An intake of breath can lead to an observation, a memory, and wry comment. These days of my life are simply a temporary arrangement of our energies. I could visit her grave today, and Dad's, or Mark's with his Marcy next to him, bring flowers, hang out a while. I could be quiet here at home, let the veil of remembrance fall over me, and if tears fall, they fall. ✦

RUTH SELID worked as an urban design planner in the City of Portland, retiring at 55 to travel. In August 2018, unusually exhausted from two weeks of solo travel in Croatia, she sought medical attention and was soon diagnosed with an advanced case of Myelodysplastic Syndrome. After three years of successful treatment, the cancer transformed to Acute Myeloid Leukemia. A new chemo routine is promising but rarely effective for more than two years.

Memories are Water

Memories change, unless they harden
Waves come in and waves go out
Read the river lightly, it has a life of its own
The water will teach me, if I can hear it

I can only hear it if my mind stops
and my heart starts

This is what I hear; the gurgling of insistent memories
My feelings were fear and helplessness, then

I see that day
I remember the bright, full October sky
Puffy from all the saline, blood, and magnesium infused into me
I was standing there frozen, a shred of myself

I don't need to write about the pain of previous Octobers
The river current is forcing my hand across the page
It is rattling me towards living

I painted a wave yesterday—a forced curl of energy
I know, without a doubt, that wave will crash
Then the water, humbled
will continue to move back out to sea

The ocean doesn't stop
Memories don't need to stay stuck

It is the most natural thing in the world
for water to keep moving ✦

Bird Shit

Bird shit! Splattered all over my car were globs and globs of white ammunition. My husband and I had just walked in a woozy-crooked sort of way across the hospital parking lot toward my bombarded car. The vehicle sat innocently under a tree. It had been there for several weeks, and it looked like the long stay annoyed the birds who lived in the tree above.

I was sure it was those big-brained crows that were responsible. They probably made it a game to find out which bird-champion could get the largest plop on the front window. The abandoned car was like a giant bull's eye for their entertainment.

My husband and I were stunned by the circumstances of our lives. The bird shit was the most recent of a series of shocking events. Everything had dramatically changed when two weeks earlier I had driven myself to the emergency room, parked under the tree, and was quickly absorbed into the hospital by my health crisis. For two weeks, I didn't even remember that I had a car, much less where I had left it parked.

We fell into the seats, bruised. When he turned the windshield wipers on, the white goo slid across the window. We watched in slow-motion horror. It smeared thickly, blurring our way forward. We looked at each other, not sure if we should laugh or cry. He squirted the windshield wiper fluid over and over as we waited.

The white sludge on my window surprisingly made things clear. There were certain lessons my husband and I were being forced to learn about the impact of this unexpected life-threatening illness. The first lesson was to acknowledge that indeed we felt we had been shat on!

Suddenly we were acutely aware that life was a big, scary mess. The goo all over my car also showed us that we were required to be patient. We had to accept the absurdities of life. We must seek and find clarity. This was the only way, if we were to see our way safely home. ✦

SALLY FOSTER RUDOLPH enjoys writing in a circle with others and on her own. She is a visual artist who likes walking her dog, and loves spending time with her family, usually on the river if the sun is shining. Sally has lived with a life-threatening illness for eight years. Sally is a board-certified and licensed art therapist. She works with hospice patients and their families using both art therapy and writing-as-therapy as means of expression.

A 60% Chance

Before diagnosis, I pulled weeds and cut back brush and planted and tended in long happy afternoons.

After diagnosis, I pull weeds and cut back brush and plant and tend in careful 30-minute segments.

Before diagnosis, I did yoga and cycled and walked.

After diagnosis, I do yoga and cycle and walk with reverence and a thankful heart.

Before diagnosis, I ate well to keep my weight down.

After diagnosis, I eat well because I honor my body as the conduit of my life.

Before diagnosis, I walked unimpeded by the possibility of illness.

After diagnosis, I walk burdened by the knowledge of illness.

Before diagnosis, I thought I didn't understand the mystery of mortality.

After diagnosis, I know I don't understand the mystery of mortality.

Before diagnosis, I had a lifetime.

After diagnosis, I have today. ✦

Heather the Tether: Reflections from an IV pole on 14K

While I appreciate your giving me a name—most don't—I also can't help but notice the sarcasm, the not-so-slight defamation of my very nature. Can I help it if my sole reason to exist is to hold these tubes and these beeping monitors above your PIC line so they can drip their magic poison in just the right amounts into your veins, thus keeping you alive?

And you call me Heather the Tether. You decorate me with fringe, causing me to look like an emaciated, metallic hula-dancer. I can't hula dance. I have no hips.

I notice that you prefer the moments when we are disconnected, and you can delight in closing the bathroom door all the way or turn over in bed without triggering an array of alarms. I take no offense. I see your mixed emotions as you walk, dragging me down the hall and around the nurse's station.

Around and around for weeks on end. Until that day—and allow me to apologize—when my wheels squeaked so loudly as we passed Stinky Mary, the nurse. Around and around we went. Squeak, squeak. Squeak, squeak. We both noticed her annoyance each time we passed. And then she snapped. She marched off to find another IV pole, one with quieter wheels. She swapped me out.

After that, I saw you as you passed by. You noticed me standing tall but alone in the alcove, my hula fringe hanging still and quiet. I noticed your glances. You missed me. I know you did. ✦

Fear of Recurrence

It's a swooshing sound. It starts as a distant beat, but experience tells me it grows and gets louder and closer. A swoosh-swoosh, swoosh-swoosh steady beat. It's so faint I hear it only rarely and only at night as sleep creeps in and drags me willingly into oblivion.

That quiet drum beat in my ears scares me to my core. It's a type of tinnitus called Pulsative Tinnitus. That there is a medical name for it brings me no relief. I first heard it weeks before my leukemia diagnosis, before I had any idea what was coming. I told my neighbors to check the well, which must be malfunctioning. I was baffled when we pulled up the floorboards of the wellhouse and found nothing. I finally put it together one day as I sat in the car on a beautiful spring day in Oregon. The sound is coming from within. It's my heartbeat.

I fear the sound is a harbinger. I heard it again late one night and fear stalked me. I stared into the darkness, certain of relapse. The next morning, I walked up the steps to my son's house. I realized how much I love walking up the stairs to his house, knowing that in a moment joyful chaos would greet me with grandchildren and dog. I choked back tears as I hugged my son. I felt acute and imminent loss.

I heard this sound again last night, uninvited and unwelcome. Still, it's helpful that I'm under the weather today. Can I redefine this Pulsative Tinnitus and connect it to something other than blood cancer? Maybe it's what my body sounds like when I don't feel well. Maybe instead of my blood being overcome, it's doing what it's meant to do—attack and defeat viruses. Maybe it's the sound of my blood cells fighting for my life, and wouldn't that make me healthy? Lucky even? Equipped for today? Maybe I could cheer this swoosh-swoosh on. Work, blood cells, work! I've got your back! Thank you! Thank you! ✦

SANDRA CLARK is a life-long educator, the grateful mother of three, and a grandmother. She was diagnosed with Acute Myeloid Leukemia in May 2019 and spent several months on 14K at OHSU. She is, as a friend observes, a rolling stone with tumbleweed roots but a sage-brush heart. She currently lives in Seattle, Washington, and advises abundant amounts of walking and writing.

Untitled

About one-third of the way in—so far, not so bad. I realized I'm less anxious about the "what-ifs," but now it's countdown to surgery. "Quasimodo" has been quiet since biopsy—really no pain or swelling like before. I think it knows what I'm doing to it. Killing it. But also taking a part of me. I didn't choose this, but now it's here, and I have to deal with it.

Who am I kidding?—I'm *still* nervous about the unknowns. Pain, prolonged healing time, possible post-surgical infection, paresthesias. These were all explained side effects, and logically I can understand and rationalize them. I'm still scared though, and that's hard to admit when I've had to be so brave thus far.

It's strange to think you can go to sleep one minute and wake up the next, and not be able to move like you once did. How does one prepare for such a change? ➤

For Sale by Owner

Barely used,

    (partially worn out)

Glitter sequin high heeled shoes.

    (uncomfortable death traps)

Worn once for a celebration,

    (kept years for no good reason)

Looking for a new home.

    (need to throw out)

Would be a great fit.

    (can't wear with an AFO) ✦

Small Stuff

The sweet taste of fresh strawberries,
Contrasted with the tartness of rhubarb;
The combination that reminds me of home.

The purring vibrations from my feline companion,
As he nuzzles his way into cuddles.
Demanding to be loved,
While loving fiercely back.

The scent of flowering trees and gardens,
The lingering fragrance temporary but beautiful.

Finally shifting focus on the here and now
And allowing myself to get lost in these moments.

I have had to focus on the future for so long:
Delayed gratification.
Cancer strangely is allowing me to slow down,
Persuading me to live. ✦

STEPHANIE BALIK was diagnosed with a soft tissue sarcoma (epithelioid malignant peripheral nerve sheath tumor) of the lower leg in June 2022. Treatment involves neoadjuvant and adjuvant chemotherapy and radiation along with surgical excision. Given the location of the tumor, surgery will remove part of the peroneal nerve, causing permanent foot drop and reliance on wearing an AFO (ankle foot orthosis) brace. Being diagnosed with cancer has overall been a humbling experience for her, as she has experienced a role shift from working as a physician to now being a patient.

This is who I am

This is who I am;

Flashing colored holiday lights.

Savoring chocolate ice cream

At 3:00 am.

Driving around in my red Honda

With my dog near me

Wearing the blue hedgehog sweater.

I smile.

This is who I am;

Eating fried rice with my sister

On a Saturday night, December upon us.

My sister is my friend.

Adulthood and parents leaving this earth

Provided spaces for growth.

This is who I am;

Digging the Earth wearing

Lime green rubber gloves.

Sitting on the ground in the sun,

My dog sprints across the yard.

The neighbor's golden lab is coming.

This is who I am;

A woman who dreams,

Awake and asleep

For the questions are endless

The answers repetitive.

This is who I am:

The person with a head of ideas

Not knowing how to spin them

Into reality when there's only

A dime in my pocket. ✦

Untitled

They all have names.

The rocks and wood

Along the sandy beaches and salty waters

Pressed into the sand by the

Tossing waves; high tides to

Low tides they remain spectators.

What stories will they tell of

Sun, storms, movement in the waves.

Do the rocks and wood know

Who the sea birds are,

Or the sand fleas, or

The stars in the sea?

And the skies that reflect

Memories that ebb and flow

Without pausing, then linger

In the sparkling grains of sand.

There are many names

In the waters, deep and liquid.

At times their voices

Attach themselves to waves

That give the ocean its roar.

Remember this while you

Observe the white crescent waves. ☝

SUSAN JOHNSON is a native of Portland, Oregon, and the Lents neighborhood. Living in the house she grew up in, she has experienced many views of change over the years. Ever since grade school, when she penned the story of *Stuart the Star*, writing has been one of her creative outlets. Poetry is her groove, especially after a breast cancer journey that began in February 2012.

come with us
and fly

The Big "C"

How did this happen?
Was it something I did?
Finally getting over these questions (which still linger from time to time)
I've realized there is no answer.
Cancer has made me more aware of my senses.
Smelling the flowers that are in season,
hearing the bird songs,
savoring the meal before me,
seeing the nature and animals on my walks,
feeling the warmth of a hug.
I didn't explore my senses before cancer,
but now I am enjoying each and every one. ✦

LINDA OMAR was diagnosed with Stage 4 colon cancer during COVID-19, in August of 2020. She has been blessed with a wonderful team of providers that have helped her work through and navigate her diagnosis. The OHSU Writing Group for Women Healing from Cancer has been a big help, as well.

Grateful and Fortunate

Many are the memories of going through the experiences after the diagnosis of breast cancer. Of course, there is the finding of a lump, the tests and the meeting with the oncologist. Somehow, I went through this part of the diagnosis in a rather calm and optimistic manner. Most of these times, I choose to forget—to put behind me as part of my move-on philosophy of life.

There is one memorable time, however, which is incredibly clear and meaningful. While I don't remember the date, I do remember the setting, where I was sitting and how I was feeling. To this day, some ten years later, it is all very clear. My chemo treatments were once a week for about three months. On Thursdays, I had the good fortune to have one of my three adult kids or best female friend take me to the infusion center. I'd be escorted in, seated, and was very comfortable and content while the healing poison flowed into my port. Covered in a nice heated blanket, I'd very peacefully fall asleep. Vividly I recall one time when my friend, Carol, took me to infusion. I awoke extremely hungry and told Carol that I was craving a steak for lunch. After driving to the restaurant, being seated with orders in front of us, I knew I was no longer hungry. After a few laughs, we packed up my uneaten lunch and was taken home. After one such treatment, I was sitting in what I called my "chemo corner" on the sofa in my living room. Suddenly, an amazingly brilliant and clear thought came to the right side of my brain, my essence, and profoundly announced, "Cancer, you are not going to get me." I knew then I'd be okay.

I had outstanding care at my hospital (Oregon Health Sciences University). From the oncologist to the surgeon to my plastic surgeon—who was not affiliated with the hospital—to the nurses and all the follow up care subsequent to the surgeries. I hear through the grapevine that after this experience, I became a "nicer" person! I expect that after a medical experience of this magnitude, one does become more grateful, aware, and compassionate. I can only hope so. How fortunate I am. Still. ⚓

GINNY McCARTHY grew up in a middle-class family in central New York. She moved to the beautiful state of Oregon in 1970, married, and has three adult children (who are scattered all over the United States, so it's a good thing they all love to travel). Ginny is now retired with lots of time to do some creative writing; but the more time there is, it seems the less time there is to write.

Instructions for Not Giving Up

After Ada Limón

When it feels impossible, go ahead and listen to the body sagging
with the heavy weight. Then take a nap to let sleep wash away the
illusion. Wake up fresh and remember all of the blessings—of running
water, of electricity, of friends. Look at the problem again. Ask for
inner guidance. Ask a friend. Take a walk. Put one foot in front of
the other as a metaphor and a reality. See which ideas present
themselves and start on the "impossible" task again and again.
Ask why it matters and see if it's time to restart or shift your energy
to a deeper why. You are more than one liter of sunlight and stardust.
The impossible will yield to you in ways you can't imagine. ✦

The Spaces Between the Stars

The spaces between sleeping and awake are filled with warm, soft breath. The spaces between each bite are full of flavor and enjoyment. The spaces between items on my list are full of mischief. The spaces between red and green at the stoplight are full of daydreams. The spaces between phone calls are full of longing. The spaces between here and there are full of twists and turns. The spaces hold all the potential for what is between the spaces. ✦

BRENDA MARKS was diagnosed with breast cancer in 2016. She is grateful that she currently has no evidence of disease after grueling chemo treatment and surgery. She lives in the Portland area and is figuring out what a post-cancer, post-pandemic life will hold.

I Wore Red

I wore red that day. I wore red and looked good! Damn good! Okay . . . that may be a stretch . . . I wore an old red t-shirt, loose around the neck so the oncology nurse could access my chemo port. I wore a matching red bandana to cover the peach fuzz that had replaced my long beautiful brown hair a few months earlier.

I was excited as I made my way up to the oncology clinic. This was my last day of chemo. My last day of putting poison into my body as part of my treatment for invasive ductal carcinoma, aka breast cancer, that I was diagnosed with in September of 2016.

After I finished the infusion, the moment all chemo patients wait for, I stepped up to ring the bell. I rang it hard to signify the end of my treatment while a multitude of pictures were taken and hugs were given.

I rang that bell that day . . . but my journey with cancer was not over.

2016 was a rough year for me. Before the breast cancer diagnosis, a hematologist diagnosed me with a rare blood cancer called Polycythemia Vera or PV. Two cancers in one year? Seriously? I thought I was healthy. How on earth could I wind up with not one, but two types of cancer?

PV causes my bone marrow to make too many red blood cells. This makes my blood thick causing severe fatigue, headaches, spleen enlargement. It also significantly increases my risk of heart attack, stroke, or blood clot. This cancer is chronic, progressive, and rare. It can't be cured, but treatment can manage it effectively.

Right now, my overall prognosis is good. Most of the time I feel okay. However, sometimes this former runner, who used to get up early to run 5 miles, struggles just to get out of bed. Sometimes fatigue hits me like a hammer. Fortunately, I have an awesome and understanding support system. For that I feel especially blessed.

I've always lived life to the fullest, but now even more so. I realize that life is finite, that I may not be around as long as I had planned. Therefore, I live large, do crazy and unusual things that are way out of my comfort zone. I try to make each day count. I am determined not to let this all defeat me or diminish my joy of life!

So why did I wear red that day? Why did I wear red on my final day of chemo? Red signifies the thick blood that runs through my veins. I wore red to symbolize the PV, the blood cancer that still continues to impact my life. I wore red to represent my never-ending cancer journey . . .

"I Wore Red" by Deb Wesloh was originally published by Health Union, LLC. on May 17, 2019. Adapted with permission. (https://blood-cancer.com/stories/ polycythemia-vera-story-2)

Contrast

I feel the sun's glowing rays caress my back like a deep relaxing massage

I feel the needle burn each time it reaches the inner layers of my skin.

    I see my skin tanned-to-perfection, a movie star shade of gorgeous brown

    I see the gruesome scars across my face, forever disfigured

    I hear the tranquil breeze as it brushes across my sunlit face

    I hear the laser with its rhythmic zapping in its futile effort to correct

I taste the light perspiration beads from above my lips

I taste the tears running down my face as I glance in the mirror, forever changed

I smell a faint scent of cocoa butter lingering in the air

I smell the sharp odor of burning flesh cauterizing the incision

Once a friend, a serene comfort

Now an enemy, a heartbreaking betrayal ✦

You Can Go

As I stood in front of an audience at the TR Ranch that brisk October evening, I thought about how life has a way of surprising you.

If you had told me five years ago that I would be on a stage singing a song to a bunch of professional singer-songwriters, I would have said you were crazy.

How did I, a rather introverted person, wind up there? Interestingly enough, I can thank cancer.

Since most of my pre-cancer activities, like running, were no longer viable, I wanted to find something to replace them. I joined a veteran songwriting group called Soldier Songs and Voices during 2019. They sponsored a songwriting event in Texas. With a love of music, I jumped at the chance to attend. I spent one of the most therapeutic weeks of my life learning the songwriting craft from some of the best.

I wanted to write an upbeat song about moving forward following a cancer diagnosis to let the world know you can overcome cancer. However, I had never attempted to write a song . . . ever. I was paired with an incredible singer-songwriter, Mary Bragg.

She asked me a little about myself and what direction I wanted to go with the song. Within thirty minutes we (and I use the word "we" loosely as Mary was responsible for the majority of it) had outlined a song and came up with a beautiful melody and lyrics. The "hook" of the song, as it is called in the songwriting world, was *You Can Go*.

I apparently didn't read the fine print to realize that, on the last night, I was to perform the song we wrote. Wait! What? I had never performed

live. Here they wanted me to sing in front of not only an audience . . .
but an audience of professional songwriters and singers. Yikes! But I
did it. Strangely enough, cancer has given me a sense of confidence that
I never had before. And singing . . . what an incredible rush.

It's been over two years since I had my big stage debut with *You Can Go*.
In 2022, I professionally recorded it and the song was used in a cancer
performance in May 2022 called *The Six*. In addition, *You Can Go* is one
of the tracks on the May/June 2022 *Folk Now* collaborative CD.

To all my fellow cancer survivors—You. Can. Go! ♥

"You Can Go" by Deb Wesloh was originally published by Health Union, LLC. on
October 29, 2020. Adapted with permission. (https//blood-cancer.com/living/song)

DEB WESLOH lives in Bulverde, Texas. She is married and has three boys. Deb is a
multi-cancer survivor. She was diagnosed with invasive ductal carcinoma (breast
cancer) and a blood cancer called polycythemia vera in 2016. In 2019, a dermatologist
diagnosed her with her first of many skin cancers. She is an Army Veteran, an aspiring
singer-songwriter, an author, and cancer patient advocate.

Pondering the Resilience of the Human Spirit

How many times have I been reborn?

Each day—waking from unconsciousness to alert presence?

Each evening—reviewing my adventures of the day, and how am I changed because of them?

Each addition that comes into my life—new items, new combinations, new friendships?

Each loss of something I have loved through displacement, correction, function, or death?

From answering the prophets' call: "Here am I—send me!"

Regarding a day substitute teaching in a new classroom, receiving an emergency page from a hospital.

Receiving a tax or Medicare client to counsel and assist.

To singing in a choir, sitting on a board of directors, or writing music . . .

How about receiving new hip replacements 22 years ago, allowing me to walk again?

Or going through rigorous cancer treatment: chemo, surgery, chemo again, and surviving . . .

Then thriving and finding new interests like art, poetry and creative writing.

Now needing hip revision surgery, even through robustness and fortitude.

Let's take care of them while you are well and strong and young . . .

The surgery will be easier, and your recovery more complete.

Think of it like replacing a fan belt in your car before it wears out.

There's an important part in your hips that have worn very thin.

We're doing this because we expect you to live a long time.

From denial to acceptance—that has also been my story of rebirth.

Now, surgery—just three days away for the right hip—things have fallen into place.

Support people, an organized safe home, walkers, and crutches.

Everything in line, prepped, prepared, first my things, and then gradually my mind and my emotions.

The resiliency of the human spirit—this new next adventure.

Preparing me, as was said, *For the next 22 years!*

Yes, I say—*Yes again*—*YES!* ✦

"Grace"—My New Middle Name

Grace—looking back at my life so far—almost 70!

I see how very much grace has offered her kindness.

Having a teaching job that transitioned easily into a retirement substitute job.

Being on the cusp of chaplain work through previous volunteer work, then residency.

Being at the right place at the right time to train to become our congregation's Para-Rabbinic assistant.

Finding my place because of previous interests, to offer assistance in tax, Medicare, music, and other counseling and therapies to my community.

Having incredible primary care providers, oncologists, orthopedic surgeons, dentists, naturopaths, acupuncturists, and other health providers

That have allowed me to age gracefully, wondrously, and with agility.

Having rabbis who have been so supportive, making my way easy no matter what came along.

Having loving, supportive family and friends that volunteer and are easily there for me when I need them.

Having enough funds in my life to have vacations, holidays, and travel.

Always having reliable transportation, so that spontaneous work anytime, day or night, is possible and enjoyable.

Having a quick mind—so that opportunities that show themselves can be incorporated as needed or wanted.

Living comfortably, even with major challenges, and filling my home with delights for my senses.

Having the ability and training to create, teach, play, sing, and enjoy beautiful music.

Having interests, hobbies, and the initiative to continually find expansion in my world.

So very much Grace! Blessings and Grace to All! ✾

JUDITH KLEINSTEIN lives in Portland, Oregon. She has had bilateral hip replacements, and 22 years later, bilateral hip revisions. She has been treated for several recurrences of ovarian cancer, and recently had a chest port placed as she began treatment for another recurrence. She is an active substitute teacher, hospital chaplain, traveler, and community volunteer.

The Japanese Gardens

The treatments have flushed me. Where are the guides on these paths?
Who are my guides now?
Wandering through the Japanese Gardens, I look to see something new
each day, savoring a blossom, noticing a new shadow as sunlight sneaks
through the trees.

An old bonsai tree is on display—small, compact, but oh so strong,
fierce against the elements. I am like that sometimes.

The koi in the pond are mentors for modeling how to slow down. Languid
swimmers, they move together and alone. Barely touching, they are
brilliant: gold, black, white, and orange. Round and round they go each
morning. Here I can take a deep breath; my mind slows way down. I try
to hold onto that as I move through my day.

Traveling on the same paths and noting daily changes forces me to pay
attention! Notice! Look! See!

There is no rushing here. There is only meandering along the path,
walking up and down the stone steps. The path is a guide. There are many
lessons from the koi and the flowing water. Slow down; treasure the time.

Gardens as guidance
Meandering pathways
Leading me to health, hope, and life ✦

Cancer as a Change Agent

Cancer and COVID have been gigantic change agents for me to slow down, pay attention, and have more gratitude for what used to be the ordinary, the everyday.

I try each morning to write a gratitude list. It can be too easy to spiral down. I can fall into despair and hopelessness given the small circle of my life. It then can spiral out to a larger circle of negativity. I must hold on to those bigger ideas, look towards the North Star, and find inspiring people.

Mr. Rogers said his mother told him to look for the helpers.

Mahatma Gandhi said, "When I despair, (*Wow! Even Gandhi despaired at times!?*) I remember that all through history the way of truth and love have always won. There have been tyrants and murderers, and for a time, they can seem invincible, but in the end, they always fall. Think of it—always."

So helpful . . . Because sometimes in the middle of the night I get scared, very scared. Despair in the darkness goes deeper than that of the daylight.

Each day is another gift. Truly my two cancers have taught me that and continue to teach me again and again. The voices of loved ones who have passed on remind me, too. The daily lessons are: Slow down! Appreciate! Savor this day!

It is what I have. ✘

DEBORAH COLETTE MURPHY was born in New York City but now lives down a dirt road in the woods of Southern Oregon. Deborah has been a teacher of children and college students for decades. She loves reading, writing, traveling, and having FUN! She tries to treasure every day as a gift.

MARY ELLEN BOLES

Time

time is a placeholder
standing still or speeding forward
even moving backwards
until the only way i know
i'm not 16 is to look in the mirror.
a reminder that 52 years have flown
and i am not the girl with the easy laugh
and soft lips primed
for hours of lying in the grass
kissing until my face is chapped
and i am an hour past curfew.

how can there be such discord
between the face the world sees
and what i feel inside.

i carry the ghosts of then
faded photos of parties and laughter.
a carefree simplicity we
didn't value or even recognize.
lifelong friendships
dissolved only by death.
there are still a few of us.
standing
thriving even
as we enter another summer
of our winter years.

Walk with me

Walk with me Grandma, as you did when my children were born. Bring your daughter, my mother. Invite my father and brother, my aunts, uncles, cousins, great-grandparents, all those whose blood I share. We are connected drop by drop.

Your DNA drives mine, as mine will continue to drive those who come after. Walk with me, hold my hand. Steady my step when I falter. Strengthen my gait when it grows weak. Whisper in my ear as a remembrance I am not alone. Encourage when fear has me frozen. Plant a song when music has grown faint. Pray for me when I have forgotten how.

When darkness threatens to smother, help me find the light. Guide me toward the warmth of the sun, the beauty of the stars, the light of the moon. Help me retain my sense of humor, my ability to smile when I have lost both. Show me a poem or assist me in writing one when the power of words has left. Remind me how much I am loved and how many I love when I cloak myself in despair and hopelessness, when I choose self-pity over gratitude, when I bathe in pain instead of beauty. Pierce open my heart with your love. Everyday. ✦

MARY ELLEN BOLES is moving toward retirement, finding a new path in the chaos of recent years. She writes, walks, reads, explores, and visits with loved ones, finding comfort in the gifts of such simplicity.

Untitled

intuition
is

the
clarity
and
honesty

courage
and
confidence

to
embrace

wisdom
and
harmony

that
leads

to
the
inspiration

creativity
and
trust

to
express

one's
truth ✦

Laughing

a
belly
shaking
laugh

vibrating
my
entire
body

penetrating
the
room

filling
it

with
goodness

the
sweetest
medicine
ever

laughing
saved
my
life

Fairy Godmother with Turquoise Hair
La Fata Turchina

did
I
become
her?

or

was
I
her
all
along?

stumbling
and
stumbling

smoothing
and
smoothing

radiance

more
and
more

vibrant
than

I
ever
imagined

growing
youthful
in
spirit
and
older
in
soul

I
am
the
Fairy Godmother with Turquoise Hair

creating
and
celebrating

enchantment
miracles
and
love ✦

Poet, Singer, Dancer, and Storyteller, **REINA SOFIA DE LA LUZ** explores a variety of modes of artistic expression. A poet since childhood, she is eager to share her heart's creations with you.

ROBBIN ISAACSON DeWEESE

Qualities

Commitment:

She committed herself to figuring out how to spell commitment, committing, committed, committee. Double Ms? Double Ts? Even double Es!

She married him, committing herself to a shared life with this wonderful person she loved. Later, she chose to not dye her graying hair. One life commitment was enough.

She found meaning in the Tuesday morning cancer writing support group, yet also committed to helping in an early morning English language class.

Without considering the hurt her choices might cause, she committed some major faux pas.

Boredom:

A choice that can be remedied. Though sometimes it can be challenging to find a way out. Imagination and creativity can address boredom.

Practice:

She's learning to see things she does as practice. Yoga practice, painting practice, writing practice. It's never an accomplishment, just something you keep doing. When she was young, she thought if you went to dance class or yoga class or any class you would learn to dance or paint, play clarinet, do yoga or math, and then you'd know it. As a kid she hated school and wished for a knowledge pill you could just swallow to learn whatever you were supposed to know. It's taken a long time to understand it doesn't work that way! Practice makes perfect is an unreachable goal. Practice is just practice. There is no perfect, only practice. Habits are what's important. ➤

Body!

Awakening each day, I stretch out of bed,

see my feet, ankles, calves, knees, thighs.

Good Morning Amazing Body!

Soon you will be embraced in pants

and I'll feel you carrying me on my daily walk.

I'm here breathing in dogwood pink,

Rhody's vibrant reds and purples,

shades of green budding leaves.

Greeting the day and the people I see.

ROBBIN ISAACSON DeWEESE delights in her retirement from a fulfilling career as a language teacher. She is grateful for the love of family, friends, and medical support team who smoothed her cancer experience, and for the able body she awakes to every morning. Robbin spent her childhood in New Orleans and her adulthood in Portland. Between this wonderful writing group, painting class, yoga, cooking, long walks, and time with dear ones, she wonders how she ever had time to teach.

SABRINA NORRIS McDONALD

Hands of Grace

The sleep of surgery went quickly for her, but the ten and a half hours for me and the four other surgeons were grueling and, at times, precarious. I am trained for this and have performed countless surgeries, but this one was especially complex. Knowing now her spirit and her family, I left little pieces of myself in the sutures. And in the void of her belly, I placed a prayer. ✦

In utmost gratitude to Dr. George J. Chang, colorectal surgical oncologist, MD Anderson Cancer Center, Houston, Texas.

The Dance Floor

I wanted to think that acceptance was linear, like a garden gate
I could walk through just once and be free. But as it turns out,
the gate is an illusion.

My challenges are ever present, always evolving, and float invisibly
on the wind until they brush up against my face or hand as I round
the corner of a building, raise a glass of cold milk to my lips, turn on
my left turn indicator in my car, or close my eyes at day's end.

Like uninvited guests at a dance party, Sorrow and Anger follow me
around asking for spots on my dance card. I often pretend I don't see
or hear them. Anger is easily distracted and moves on to find other
dance partners if I refuse. But Sorrow . . . Sorrow is more persistent. She
follows me and hides under food tables, underfoot, or under the folds
of my dance skirt. Saying no to Sorrow never banishes her. I may as
well dance with her so that I can move on my way. She leads, I follow.
The music is long and slow but eventually fades along with Sorrow.
We have danced together many times, and I know we will meet again
when it suits her.

Until then, I find a quiet spot to rest for a while with a cool cup of water.
In due time, a lively tune will pull me back to the dance floor. For I know
the dancing never ends. And my card is open. ❣

Dear Friend,

*—Upon learning of the passing of our collective
sister/daughter, our Kelly Walsh*

So stunned, distraught, and distracted by the news of your passing I
have been, that I almost missed you there outside my bedroom window.

I've always marveled at the perpetual mystery of how the dead and
even the dying can come to our aid and comfort in the midst of the
chaos of their own transformations.

But there you are!

Here you are!

Right here with me!

You are the emerald green of the new spring growth of the black ash
above me. Your leaves spin chartreuse as the spring sun illuminates
them from above on this May morning. You are waving to me. I can see
you smile there in the waving leaves as you dance in the warm sunlight.
You jump, weightless, from branch to branch, chasing sunbeams
through the canopy.

Oh, my! How easily you move into the chickadee to chatter with your
avian friends, who are like us. And now, you have slid into the sparkling
water of the bird bath. You splash them as they play in your coolness.
Soon you become a new bunny among the others. They scamper with
delight at the arrival of a new playmate. Your downy brown fur blows in
the breeze as you romp through the tall grasses. I hear your laughter
in the chase.

But wait, how have you traveled so deftly, so freely to the first red roses below my window?

So, is THIS how it is? And has it always been so, while we mortals waste our precious lives worrying that we would end?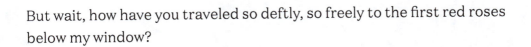

SABRINA NORRIS McDONALD began life as a Texan but has now lived over half her life in Oregon. She loves all things in the natural world, enjoys connections with friends, family, strangers (strangers are just friends you haven't met yet), and animals. Creating is what keeps a smile on her face and a jig in her step.

The Miracle of Existence

—2020, after Walt Whitman

Sing and dance ! Find some joy !

Have a good belly laugh with a few people !

Spend a moment in the Sun

Feel the energy of Source filling you up with its golden glow

Walk in the woods and sit in front of a tree

Feel the force of Life driving the sap, moving energy and nutrients

Skywards

Put your bare feet on the ground and grow roots into the earth

Let her give you the sustenance and nourishment for creation

Be stupid & Crazy & Uneducated !

Travel ! Discover ! Question !

Free yourself from prejudice and thoughts that are not yours

Look for questions, not answers

For nothing is truly known nor fully understood

This lack of knowledge is freedom !

Stay young in heart and mind !

Explore your consciousness through fresh perceptions and senses

Reach through the veil to reveal pure radiant emptiness

Most of all, see the Beauty and Love

in all things, and be grateful for

the miracle of existence.

At the water's edge

—April 22, 2020

Come with me to the boundary
Here at the water's edge
Peer out into the ocean
Look down at the riverbed
Listen to the conversation
Of liquid talking to solid,
Of water pushing into the land
The dynamic erosion of the earth
Bubbling in the foam of ocean waves
Gurgling in the rapids and waterfalls,
Energy that shapes and sculpts,
Nourishing the chemistry of life
The crashing of rocks, the chatter of pebbles
The murmur of the sand
Ground eternally finer and smoother
By the great wheel of time

The thunder of crashing breakers
Relentlessly pounding rocky cliffs
Hammering out beautiful stone arches
Until they crumble and fall.

A Wave Blanket

—December 2019

Soothed by the Sea
Warmed by a Wave
The roaring surf a lullaby,
the foam a fizzy blanket.
Water washing over me,
asleep on the soft sand.
Out of the chaos, tranquility emerges . . .
Bringing me peace as I find my role
Seeming insignificant
But essential for the whole
A drop of water in the ocean,
on the beach a grain of sand.
One human among billions,
across the seas, in distant lands.
The ocean and beach sing together
Locked in an eternal dance
I linger in their embrace
Comfortable in my place
Feeling Snug ~ Feeling Safe

SEAN HOOVER (1986–2021) gives meaning to the words "we are made of stardust." A scientist, a mystic, a warrior, and above all, a friend. A lover of music, books, laughter, and learning, his presence still transmits a deep desire for sharing his knowledge and joy for life. You can sense this in his writing, especially in his poetry. He took to writing when joining the OHSU Writing Group for Young Adults Healing from Cancer with Brianna and Juliana, with whom he developed a deep friendship. Sean continued to touch more lives later as others joined the group. Sean died at the age of 34 in May of 2021, after living with leukemia on and off for six years.

I Can

It's not what I can't do that counts.

It's what I can!

I can

Go to my senses.

I can see the magical color of a Mikado rose petal blend seamlessly
from red to cerise to orange to the glow of fire at the center.

I can savor the pungence of evergreens dominating a ferment of loam
in the forest.

I can feel the warmth of spring sunshine soothe the ache of winter
from my shoulder blades.

I can feel the ermine silkiness of a cat's paw.

I can listen actively and deeply for the essence of what is being said to me.

I can tune into the chirp, buzz, whir, and rustle of life around me
in the garden.

I can marvel at the twitchy, warm velvet of a Mustang's muzzle.

When I am tuned into my senses, I am full of wonder, curiosity, and joy.

I can delight someone precious to me with a home-crafted gift.

I can surprise with a discerning question or an appreciative comment.

I can discover color as a medium for play and exult in the burst of joy that watercolor experimentation cleanses me with.

I can create a gastronomic experience for the tongue and nose and nurture the health of the whole.

I can experiment with new expression in art, writing, and friendships.

I can take joy in movement to express myself and to accomplish tasks.

I can be vulnerable and let the chips fall where they may and know that how another responds is not about me but about them.

I can choose to trust because only I can hurt my soul.

I can write because it's for me, and if others get value, bravo.

I can create for the exquisite joy of expression.

I can invent to solve problems.

I can delight in the achievements of my grandkids and their parents.

My life is a blessing I choose to exult in. These deaths and cancer do not define me. I am not broken. I am whole.

I CAN

The Tipping Point

I am in the primordial battle of my life—Fear versus Passion.

If I buy into my fears and let fear determine my every move, I will climb into a hole and isolate, and the fear hormones will eat like acid on every fiber of health I have left, and I will die.

If I choose meaning, purpose, and passion to express my creative, intuitive, bold, innovative, authentic self, my vital forces will swarm to mend and heal all aspects of my mind and body.

I can rise from these ashes of death and make the world my playground and the world's creatures my playmates. ⨏

TRISH COFFEY was born in 1943 and raised on four continents and in 23 countries. She delights in weekly calls from three continents and nine states. The world is her playground, and plants and animals are her playmates.

99 Percent

I went to see a general surgeon about having a growth removed from my shoulder. All summer I had been regaining my strength and equanimity after making the difficult decision to leave a job I no longer loved. The slight swelling bugged me. *Why not get it removed?* I thought. I felt vain but tried to justify a snip of self-improvement.

A massage therapist saw it first. Almost certainly a benign lipoma, he said. Yes, my oncologist agreed, just a lipoma. Then the careful surgeon, reviewing my cancer history, shifted his focus from shoulder to breast to conduct an exam. Oh!

"I'm 99 percent sure," he said on finding a new lump, "that this is a cyst. But I want you to get an ultrasound." A couple of panicked hours later, smearing cold gel around, the radiologist said, "I'm 99 percent sure this is not a cyst. I want to send a biopsy to the pathologist. To be sure."

That 99 percent thing. Is that a bad-news technique doctors learn? To dunk you in fresh horror like a teabag, the mass sinking below the boiling water, only the thin cotton string dangling above you? That one percent your link back to the world you occupied just a moment ago, a thread too slim to climb or cling to, too fragile to pull you back out, its only function to swish you in hot hell until your old, safe self is fully steeped in this bitter brew?

So began my return to cancer-land, a place I left nine years earlier and felt was finally behind me. Uprooted? Picture a sturdy Douglas fir flipped on its side by a rough coastal storm, its heavy anchors now ripped from the foundational soil of its life, that huge root ball still gripping rocks and dirt and smaller plants in the claws that had held it firmly upright in the earth for decades. Now rawly exposed, you can see what kept it attached, settled and strong, for so long. That seam—there, in the air—between the seen and the unseen. ✦

Wild Around the Edges

Fifteen years after my first cancer diagnosis and seven years after my second, these two death threats hover, advancing and retreating, rousing me.

I write to locate my story. But what words belong to it? None of the standard cancer tropes have resonated with me. When speaking with friends, family, and doctors, I squirmed with discomfort as they employed the usual metaphors.

"Fighting back"? Of course I hated what was happening to me. And yet the disease was in my body, and I didn't wish to embitter myself further by making my own flesh the enemy. So, not a battle.

"Finding the silver lining"? Of course my priorities were instantly clarified: life paramount, love animating, time limited. Everything else negotiable or beneath consideration. Isn't that always how it is? Isn't the diagnosis but a loud reminder? And yet to couple *cancer* with *gratitude* seemed a demonic pairing at worst, a treacly sympathy card at best. So no, not a wake-up call.

"Following the journey"? Of course both yearlong treatments took me to unexplored places the way travel does, but mine felt more like a forced march. I had neither compass nor map to guide me; no thirst for wonders along the way; and, like a seasick sailor, my only desired outcome was for the trip to be over. So I rejected the journey language, too.

Instead, by the time I was ready to make art from my experience I needed to tear language apart; to shred words into bits; to reassemble them into never-before-seen images. I was a pointillist constructing a collage, the kind where no individual color represents an eye or a nose until it discovers its place in the face it is creating.

If a new countenance arose from these scraps, I wanted to meet her. Cancer could go now. I would become a new story, alive at the core and wild around the edges. ⋎

Come With Us and Fly

In my dream, the birds landed while I was sleeping. I did not know they were there. But something woke me. Maybe the soft rustling of their wings. Maybe little cooing sounds. Or maybe just the presence of their lives bringing energy to the air around me.

"There is life beyond life, all around you, all the time," said the birds. "There is more life than you know. There are layers of life, within and without."

I opened my eyes.

"There is life in your sorrow," they whispered. "There is life in your joy. There is life in your confusion, your grief, your fear. Even in your dullness and apathy, even in your moments of disconnectedness, there is life."

My tears rose hot and soft—release, relief, homecoming—as the birds continued their wordsong.

"There is life because you are the seed at the center of your experience. If you open through it and into it, you will stretch and expand into even more aliveness."

Their voices dropped, low and true, the way a wise being speaks when she arrives at the heart of the matter.

"Lift yourself into all this life, as we do when we fly. Come with us and fly." ✦

BIJA GUTOFF is a writer, editor, and artist living in Portland, Oregon. In recent years, she has been exploring writing and art to help reintegrate the self after the dislocations of illness, grief, and loss.

The OHSU Knight Cancer Institute is driven by a single mission: to end cancer as we know it.

We are a team of hundreds of doctors, nurses, scientists and other professionals who have earned a national reputation for excellence. Every year, we treat about 6,000 patients and conduct about 1,400 research projects, including more than 400 clinical trials.

Our research has led to groundbreaking advances in targeted therapy, immunotherapy and other ways to fight cancer. We're also working on new ways to find cancer early, when it's easier to treat. We're working to free the world from the burden of cancer, one patient at a time.

The Patient & Family Support Services of the Knight Cancer Institute assist patients and families throughout their cancer experience with advocacy, education, resources, and compassion.